D0831669

"Want to be a better person in every area of your life? *What Would Jesus Think?* clearly and simply explains how you can experience the power of a Christ-controlled mind that will change your life from the inside out."

Warren Wiersbe
Author and conference speaker

"It shouldn't be a secret: most battles are won or lost at the thought level. Mary Whelchel explains how to take every thought captive to guarantee victory, replacing unbiblical, negative thoughts with those that are right, lovely, noble, and true. This book will be a big help to those who find themselves frustrated before they even get started."

Guy R. Doud
Author, *Living Beyond Regrets*

WHAT
WOULD
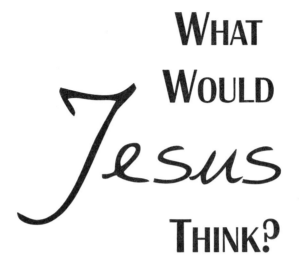
THINK?

MARY WHELCHEL

Chariot Victor Publishing
A Division of Cook Communications

ChariotVICTOR Publishing,
a division of Cook Communications, Colorado Springs, Colorado 80918
Cook Communications, Paris, Ontario, Canada
Kingsway Communications, Eastbourne, England

WHAT WOULD JESUS THINK?
© 1998 by Mary Whelchel. All rights reserved.
Printed in the United States of America

Editor: Afton Rorvik
Designer: Bill Gray
Interior Designer: Cheryl Ogletree

1 2 3 4 5 6 7 8 9 10 Printing/Year 01 00 99 98

Library of Congress Cataloging-in-Publication Data

Whelchel, Mary.
    What would Jesus think?/by Mary Whelchel.
        p. cm.
    ISBN 1-56476-697-7
    1. Thought and thinking—Religious aspects—Christianity.
2. Christian life. I. Title.
BV4598.4.W44 1998   97-44040
248.4--dc21   CIP

TABLE OF CONTENTS

Foreword

The old adage says it best, "You aren't what you think you are, but what you *think*, you are!

In this helpful book, Mary Whelchel convinces us that if we learned to think biblically, our lives would be changed by the power of God. Included are enough examples of people who have changed that even the most discouraged among us can take heart. And, best of all, she shows us how this transformation can come about.

In Bunyan's *Holy War*, a demon asks how the battle for the minds of men is to be fought. "Lies, lies, lies," Satan replied. "We must get them to accept the lies as truth." This book will help us identify the lies we have believed and show us how the truth can "set us free."

What Would Jesus Think? is a question that forces us to evaluate our thought life and responses to the haphazard events of life. Christ, is after all, not only Savior, but also our example of how to confront injustice, disappointment, and even death. From Him we learn how to face temptation, how to cope with the betrayal of a friend, and how to accept the humiliation of being misunderstood and unappreciated. From Him we also learn how to think about God, love, and enduring values. And we, as servants, should strive to think the thoughts of our Master.

We must in effect, "frisk" the thoughts that come into our minds so that we know whether they should be welcomed or not. Mary explains what the Bible means when it tells us we should dwell on things that are right and pure and lovely. And she gives us assignments that will help us solidify these ideas in our minds.

Our thinking will not be transformed by just listening to sermons, having a quick word of prayer, and trying to do better next time. The changes we seek can only be made if we take meditation and memorization of the Scriptures seriously. This book will show us how such disciplines can be done with the most profit.

I've known Mary Whelchel for more than fifteen years and rejoice in the wide ministry God has given her both in print and on the radio. Recently, she has been added to our church staff as the Director of Women's Ministries. This book bears the marks of a seasoned Christian woman who knows both the despair of defeat and the joy of freedom in Christ. Read it, do the assignments, and it might change your life.

Dr. Erwin Lutzer
Senior Pastor
The Moody Church

INTRODUCTION

This is a book that could change your life!

I recognize that is a bold statement and could certainly be construed to be a very proud and boastful claim. The life-changing potential of this book, however, has nothing to do with the fact that I've written it. In fact, my concern is that my writing may get in the way or fail to effectively communicate this profound truth.

This is a book that could change your life because it is about God's principle found in His book, the Bible. And this principle is foundational in every person's life. It absolutely does not matter whether you're young or old, a new Christian or a seasoned one, married or single, outgoing or introverted, rich or poor. Any person can benefit from the truth of this book.

I can testify from personal experience that the principle of this book is life changing. After a ten-year period of backsliding in my own life, I came back to a full commitment to Jesus Christ about fifteen years ago. Looking back I see where and how God began to drill this principle of right thinking into my life, and it has changed me in ways I never would have believed possible. I consider right thinking the single most important biblical principle that God has taught me to incorporate into my daily life, and when I live by this principle (and I don't always), it is life changing on a daily basis.

The title *What Would Jesus Think?* reminds us that to think on things that are true, noble, right, pure, lovely, and admirable is to think as Jesus would. New Age teaching tells us to believe that we can be anything we want to be and change anything we want to change simply through our mental powers. We must always be careful not to indulge in such bloated and proud thinking. Instead, we need to ask ourselves daily, "What would

Jesus think?" and focus on right thinking as presented in God's Word.

It is equally important that we do not allow humanistic philosophies to steal what has been given to us by God's Spirit in His Word. The Bible warns us that our mental attitudes and thought patterns greatly affect what we do, how well we do it, how healthy our relationships are, how fully we reach our God-given potential, and how effective we are for Jesus Christ.

Why This Book?

I've had this book in my heart and mind for a few years, but have hesitated to finalize it because I know few people will go into a bookstore looking for something to help them with their thought life. Most people don't feel the need to change their thought patterns. A book on healing past hurts touches a "felt need"; a book on improving relationships hits a "felt need" on the head. Those are the kinds of books many of us would grab and read if we truly believed they would help us.

Right thinking, however, is probably the greatest inner need most of us have, whether or not we feel it. And interestingly, dealing with any "felt need" must begin with right thinking. So, if you're thumbing through this book to see if it is relevant to your life, I can assure you it is, even if it doesn't immediately tug on your heartstrings.

The Book's Design

To try to enhance the presentation of this biblical principle and to make it as easy to understand and apply as possible, I've included a section at the end of each chapter entitled **"Think About It!"** This section will help you get more involved with the ideas in each chapter, and it will give you some practical methods for putting those ideas to work in your life. It also can be used for group discussions or exercises.

Obviously, you are free to use this book as it suits you. But I encourage you to get involved with it, as you would an interactive software program. The more you make yourself think about what you're thinking about, the more you will be able to tap into the life-changing power of this incredible, biblical truth.

The Book's Benefits

Jesus told us that the truth will set us free (John 8:32); therefore it must also be true that error entraps us and puts us in bondage. The truth of this book—which is God's truth, not my opinion—will set you free. Is there bondage in your life, such as fear, worry, obsessions, addictions, laziness, lack of discipline, negativity, etc.? If so, you are not free to run the race set before you; you are not realizing your potential in the kingdom of God. You are settling for mediocrity and passionless living.

Jesus said He came to bring us life "to the full" (John 10:10), but sadly all too many believers miss that full life. Why? I believe we frequently miss this kind of life because we have not been set free from the bondage of our own self-controlled thinking.

If you're tired of the ups and downs of your own life as a believer and you're ready to live life to the full, then this book is definitely for you. The most you have to lose is a few hours of reading time, and the potential of what you could gain from learning and incorporating this principle can only be measured in eternal currency. It is far beyond gold or silver or worldly success.

Proverbs 16:20 tells us that "Whoever gives heed to instruction prospers." The instruction in this book on right thinking will bring you prosperity of soul; a richness in your spirit; a fullness in your daily life; an abundance of the most valued possessions in this world: peace, contentment, purpose, and joy. That is my promise, based on the authority of God's Word, not empty clichés. Give it a try! You have nothing to lose but bondage.

Chapter 1

You Are

What You Think

"For as he thinketh in his heart, so is he."

Proverbs 23:7 (KJV)

I want to tell you the experience of my friend, John, from Fresno, California. He is a single man now in his forties, who is a librarian in a large public school. John, like most of us, has long wanted to find the right mate, get married, and have a wonderful Christian home. But somehow that right person just hasn't materialized yet.

In 1990 John was fairly depressed over a recent breakup with a girlfriend of three years. It seemed his hope of marriage was dashed again, and he found himself mired in self-pity, worry, and depression.

His mom had become a regular listener to my radio program, and through that she ordered a Bible study I've written titled *The Freedom of a Captive Mind*. Seeing her son struggle with this latest disappointment in his life, she gave him a copy of the Bible study, hoping it might help bring him out of the *blues*.

John began to consider seriously the principles of that study—the same principles that I am trying to communicate in this book. That he could actually control his thought life was a revolutionary idea for him. As John puts it: *I thought I was stuck with those pink elephants in my mind.*

John told me, "If I was down on a given day, I thought, well, that's just the way I'm going to be today. I was a victim of my thought life."

Gradually, he began to understand and put into practice the principles of biblical thinking. The changes that took place in his life have amazed him. By learning to replace wrong thoughts with right thoughts, John has found freedom from those weekend depressions. Friday nights often used to be the beginning of a weekend pity party for him, but now John's weekends are full of meaningful activity. Worry about the future, about getting too old to be married, about whether or not God has someone special for him used to fill his mind much of the time, but now he has learned to refocus his thoughts, reminding himself: *Look what God is doing for me now! And look at the new people and opportunities God is bringing into my life each weekend—in fact, every day.*

Learning how important it is to control the input into his mind, because that controls his thoughts, John has found great freedom from the impure sexual thoughts and desires with which he used to struggle. He now prevents the pervasive sexual messages of the world from getting into his mind by very carefully screening what he watches on television, carefully choosing what movies he views, listening to good books on tape, and listening to contemporary Christian music rather than secular music. "Seeing and hearing sexual and romantic images only filled my mind with longings I could not rightly fulfill. Thus, they left me ultimately frustrated. I have found life so much easier and sweeter by focusing on the many wonderful things God has given me now and trusting Him with the future," John says.

I asked him recently, "Where would you be today if you had not learned and applied these biblical principles to your life?" Without hesitation he said, "I'd still be experiencing the ups and downs of my life; I'd be moody; I wouldn't work as hard as I do because I'd be spending a lot of my time thinking about things that are unproductive, or dreaming about a girlfriend that doesn't exist. I would have missed so many wonderful opportunities that God has brought my way."

John continued, "I hate to think where I would be if I hadn't learned this principle. As you start to learn the habit of focusing on God and seeing Him work, you start to realize how stupid you are if you keep thinking wrong thoughts."

What John has discovered is that the more he practices these principles on a daily basis—the more he seriously thinks about what he thinks about—the easier it becomes. He's hooked, he says, because his life is so much better in every way. He would never go back to the old John who was held captive by his own thoughts.

John is not a celebrity nor anyone famous. He has no horrible past or unusual present circumstances. He's a regular guy, with the same kind of struggles and problems in his life that most of us have. Now that he has begun to examine his thought life and conform his thoughts to biblical guidelines he has discovered a whole new world of opportunity and real joy and excitement in his life.

I'm praying with all my heart that as you begin your journey through this book, God will work the same miracle in your life.

Why We Don't Think about Our Thought Life

The importance of what we think has not been lost on the secular world, on people who have no idea what the Bible has to say about our thoughts. Psychologists, psychiatrists, doctors, educators, writers, and many others have all given testimony to the fact that the thought processes of a person are the real breeding grounds for behavior, good and bad. And many have used this knowledge to their own advantage.

It would seem that the secular world has been more adept at using this truth—you are what you think—than those of us who are born from above. Any number of secular mind-control philosophies and cults focus on gaining control of a person's mind. New Age dogma is replete with mind-control messages. Yet, amazingly few born-again believers have ever given serious thought or dedication to the pursuit of controlling their thought life. Why not? Good question. Here are some of the answers.

It never occurred to us!

I truly believe one of the major reasons many of us haven't done anything about our thought life is that it just hasn't occurred to us that our problems and their solutions begin in our mind. I suppose this is because we feel our thoughts are private. After all, thoughts don't hurt people; thoughts don't upset people; thoughts are harmless—right?

Wrong, of course. Thoughts are the birthplace of every evil act. Take the hardest, most evil criminal you can find, and if you can get into his mind and change the way he thinks, you can turn that criminal into a peace-loving, law-abiding, compassionate person who becomes an asset to society. Conversely, if you don't change that criminal's thinking, all the programs and rehabilitation and counseling in the world will have no lasting effect.

Bill Marriott of the Marriott Corporation is quoted as saying, "We don't hire people and ask them to be nice; we hire nice people." Smart man. He knows how difficult it is to try to change the way people think and make them into good employees. But if they have that kind of intention to begin with, then they can learn and grow and be productive employees.

Only one person can change your way of thinking—and you look at him or her in the mirror every morning. Ask yourself these questions: Have I ever seriously thought about my thought life? Have I ever said, *My problem is I'm not thinking right?* Have I ever launched a campaign to correct my wrong thinking and make sure it conforms to God's Word? How much have I even thought about my thoughts?

If we all answered those questions candidly, I believe the majority of us would have to say, *No, I've never really given my thoughts much thought.* We can't begin to control our thoughts until we have taken the time to examine them.

It sounds like a false religion.

Because the enemy of our faith is the father of all lies, he has done a masterful job of mixing truth and error, thus tripping up many people. Thinking positively and correctly and controlling your mind is a biblical doctrine, but New Age messages and liberal psychobabble have stolen this truth and often corrupted it with humanistic philosophy that is antibiblical. I think that has frightened some believers and kept them from even considering the Bible's teaching on mind control.

We don't know how.

Another obstacle to right thinking is that we don't know how to do it. Even those who have realized the importance of their thought life are often perplexed about the solution. How do you change the way you think? How do you get rid of harmful thought patterns? How do you stop thinking the wrong kind of thoughts?

God's Word is clearer and has more information on this topic than on many other issues we face on a daily basis. The road you take to biblical thinking is a clearly marked path, with lots of warning signs and plenty of directions all along the way. Anyone who wants to search the Bible for answers will find them there without a great deal of trouble.

I've found, however, that often we are just not adept at taking biblical principles and applying them in our day-to-day lives. We don't always know how to take the words off the pages of the Bible and turn them into everyday realities.

It sounds different and difficult.

Another hurdle we find on the road to right thinking is that it seems very different. It seems that way because it is that way. Isaiah put it right:

"For my thoughts are not your thoughts, neither are your ways my ways," declares the Lord. "As the heavens are higher than the earth, so are my ways higher than your ways and my thoughts than your thoughts."

Isa. 55:8-9

Anything different is frightening; anything different requires change; anything different seems difficult at first. But God's ways, though different, are always much easier and less complicated than our ways.

If we would know freedom from the wrong thinking that has infested our minds, we must be willing to go God's way and abandon ourselves to His method, even though at times it will seem ridiculous, too tough, unreasonable, unsophisticated, unnecessarily restrictive, and/or boring! So the first thought we have to change is this mistaken idea that God's ways are too hard or too painful or too dull. None of that is true; God's ways are just different from our ways.

Why We Must Think about Our Thought Life

Now that we have explored at least some of the reasons why we don't examine our thoughts, let's take a look at the reasons why we must do so.

We must keep Satan from gaining a foothold.

Did you know that there is a great battle going on to capture your mind? The god of this present age, Satan, is doing everything possible to control your mind. And he is an expert at it. With the multimedia available to him today, his job is easier than ever, and he's more effective than ever.

Every warrior has a tactical plan, a way to defeat his enemy. What kind of tactics does your enemy use against you in this battle for your mind? Let me mention a few.

Human logic and rationale

I've noticed how easy it is for me to start down a path of human logic, taking one step at a time, each seemingly reasonable and rational, and ending up at a conclusion that is decidedly not scriptural. Satan is smart enough not to be blatant in his schemes. He often deceives through the use of logic.

The influence of those around us

We have a tendency to be easily intimidated and influenced by others, especially if we are in the minority. If people around you hold ideas that are not biblical, you know how easy it is to agree with their beliefs for fear of being different.

The proliferation of information today

While it has its positive effects, the abundance of information in our society also has its negative effects on our thinking, if we're not careful. Think of how much more information is available to you on a daily basis versus the amount of information your parents had access to when they were your age. We are bombarded with news, with other people's interpretations of events, with lies carefully wrapped in pleasant sounding words. From birth our children are exposed to the lies of the Enemy, infiltrating their minds from every direction. He is, after all, a master liar, and he uses that tactic against us through media and the written page in the most clever ways.

Why do you suppose the Enemy of your soul wants to capture your mind? He wants to capture your mind because he knows that what you think is what you are. If he can get you to think improperly, he knows you'll also act improperly, which means he has diminished your effectiveness for Jesus Christ.

Many times the Bible uses warfare as an analogy of the Christian's daily life. For example:

When I want to do good, evil is right there with me. For in my inner being I delight in God's law; but I see another law at work in the members of my body, waging war against the law of my mind and making me a prisoner of the law of sin at work within my members.

Rom. 7:21-23

Dear friends, I urge you, as aliens and strangers in the world, to abstain from sinful desires, which war against your soul.

1 Peter 2:11

Fight the good fight of the faith.

1 Tim. 6:12

I have fought the good fight, I have finished the race, I have kept the faith.

2 Tim. 4:7

Warfare is the appropriate analogy for this battle we face when we decide to get serious about our thoughts. You will find it to be a daily battle to bring your thought life under God's control. But like any battle, this one is winnable with the right weapons and the right strategy. God has provided everything we need to have victory in this mental battle. We must learn how to effectively use our weapons and march forward to claim our victory in Christ Jesus.

Our thoughts control our lives.

Another very important reason to get to work on our thought life is that our thoughts control us.

We often say, "I believe that with all my heart." Of course, we don't literally believe with our organ known as the heart, but we use that term to indicate the true inner person. The actual believing is done in our mind, but somehow to say, "I believe that with all my mind" doesn't carry quite the same impact as saying, *I believe with all my heart*. We instinctively understand this.

Jesus said, "Blessed are the pure in heart, for they will see

God" (Matt. 5:8). That could be phrased this way: *Happy are those who have purity of mind and thought, for they will be able to see and know God.*

Jesus also warned us about the evil that comes from our heart/mind:

> For from within, out of men's hearts, come evil thoughts, sexual immorality, theft, murder, adultery, greed, malice, deceit, lewdness, envy, slander, arrogance and folly. All these evils come from inside and make a man "unclean."
>
> Mark 7:21-22

If we could wipe out all the evil in that list, we could transform our world. And all that evil begins in our hearts/minds, in our inner person.

Proverbs 4:23 tells us, "Above all else, guard your heart, for it is the wellspring of life." Out of your heart—your mind—everything else flows. It's all in your mind!

Our thoughts affect society.

Another reason why we must think carefully about our thoughts is because each individual's thought life contributes to the kind of society in which we live. The Apostle Paul warned us about thinking and how it affects our society: *For although they [wicked and godless men] knew God, they neither glorified him as God nor gave thanks to him, but their thinking became futile and their foolish hearts were darkened* (Rom.1:21). (Did you notice how Paul connects thinking—a function of the mind—with the heart?)

In this passage Paul describes the thinking of these people as futile, which means incapable of producing any result; ineffective, useless, not successful. As a result of that futile—or ineffective—thinking, these people sinned. Paul's laundry list of their sins includes everything from gossip to sexual impurity to idolatry, ruthlessness, and greed. (See Romans 1:21-32.)

Sin begins with wrong thinking. Righteousness begins with right thinking. Goodness in our society begins with individual right thoughts. Evil in our society begins with individual wrong thoughts. Sociologists and others sometimes want us to believe that evil is the result of our environment or lack of education or role models or inadequate parenting. They don't want to admit that evil is a part of human nature.

In his letter to Titus Paul wrote:

> To the pure, all things are pure, but to those who are corrupted and do not believe, nothing is pure. In fact, both their minds and consciences are corrupted. They claim to know God, but by their actions they deny him. They are detestable, disobedient and unfit for doing anything good.
>
> Titus 1:15-16

As I pointed out previously, purity is a matter of the heart—the mind and thoughts of a person. Without purity of heart, or right thinking, a person's mind becomes corrupt. That corrupt thinking then creates a person who is "detestable, disobedient and unfit for doing anything good." When a society has individuals who fit this description, it is also certain to have evil, crime, and corruption of all kinds. The more we tolerate this kind of corrupt thinking, the more we become a society full of individuals "unfit for doing anything good."

Don't be fooled by the world's answer to evil. More money, better housing, improved opportunities will not make people better. While it may be good to do some of these things, the best way to change society is to help people start thinking the way God thinks, one thought at a time.

We Can Learn to Think Biblically

We are born with a tendency for evil thinking, and unless God works a miracle in our hearts and in our minds, we will find that our thinking is often not good in its natural form. Christians are just as susceptible to evil thinking as anyone else. If we do not learn and practice the biblical principles of right thinking, we will never know freedom from the sins that too often plague and defeat us.

Second Corinthians 3:18 says that we who are born from above are being transformed into the likeness of Jesus with ever-increasing glory. That's what distinguishes us from everybody else around us—we are in the process of this incredible and glorious transformation. But all too often the transformation is slow and almost undetectable because our thought lives are out of control.

As a young businesswoman, exposed to a world of materialism and greed and drive, I bought into the lie that things and relationships could satisfy me and make me happy. As a result, I spent ten years "doing my own thing" and wandering away from the biblical lifestyle and teaching that had been given to me through a wonderful Christian upbringing. The sin that resulted from this unbiblical lifestyle began with wrong thinking. Had I not started thinking unbiblically, I would never have behaved unbiblically.

Biblical Thinking Requires Discipline

I would not try to tell you that bringing your thoughts under control is a piece of cake; it is not very complicated, but it is not always easy. Nor is it a one-time effort that we can accomplish on any given day. While the Bible offers guidelines and principles that we indeed must follow, it does not offer one simple formula that can be programmed into our mental computers. Rather, bringing our thoughts under God's control must become a daily discipline, imposed and practiced with commitment and dedication.

The secret to success in this endeavor is found in 2 Corinthians 10:5: "We demolish arguments and every pretension that sets itself up against the knowledge of God, and *we take captive every thought to make it obedient to Christ.*"

Taking every individual thought captive must become our focus. We must never be lenient on ourselves. We must develop the spiritual muscle that enables us to recognize wrong thoughts quickly, grab those wayward thoughts, and snatch them back into line so that they are obedient to the principles and truth of Jesus Christ. This will require a spiritual discipline that is more demanding than the physical disciplines of keeping our bodies in good shape.

So, the challenge presented to you in this book is a significant one. You won't be able to do it on your own. You will need to depend on the power of the Holy Spirit within you, and it will require humility and much time in prayer. If you are fainthearted, you will find this discipline too demanding. If you are only halfway committed, you will give up easily. If you are looking for quick fixes, you will be disappointed. You must be willing to give complete control of your life to the sovereignty of Jesus Christ.

For those of you who are willing to pay the price of having this principle of right thinking take hold in your lives, you're in for some exciting new spiritual growth. You're going to see changes in yourself you never dreamed possible, and you'll see God work in and through you as never before.

What you will discover in the process is another one of God's incredible paradoxes: by bringing your thoughts into captivity, you will find new freedom. By becoming "narrow minded," as defined by God's Word, you will expand your universe and your potential beyond your wildest dreams. By confining your thoughts to the boundaries of biblical thinking, you will move into that abundant life Jesus came to give you. And you will wonder why somebody didn't tell you this sooner, or why you didn't listen when someone did try to tell you.

The benefits of biblical thinking far outweigh the discipline required—it's not even a contest! So, let me encourage you to stick with it and go all the way. Just remember the simple question, "What would Jesus think?" and realize He's not only the source of right thinking but the power behind it.

Think About It

Why did you choose to read this book? Check all statements that apply to you.

_____I know my thought life is out of control.

_____I wondered if my thought life was out of control.

_____I realized I don't think about what I think about—and maybe I should.

_____I'm not sure. (Think about it.)

Have you tried in the past to change your thought life?

_____Yes   _____No

If yes, what were the results? Check the most accurate response.

_____No change

_____Limited change

_____Temporary change

_____Good, lasting change

If you have never tried to change your thought life, why not?

_____It never occurred to me.

_____It sounded unrealistic.

_____It seemed too difficult.

_____I was not willing to be disciplined.

_____It sounded like New Age psychobabble.

_____I didn't know how to do it.

What results would you like to achieve by gaining more control of your thought life? Check all statements that apply.

_____I would like to worry less and trust God more.

_____I would like to reduce my stress level.

_____I would like to get rid of wrong thoughts that plague me.

_____I would like to use my mental energy and capacity better.

_____I would like to have a purer life.

Chapter 2

WHAT IS

BIBLICAL THINKING?

I am simpleminded. By that I mean I need things spelled out clearly for me; I need handles I can latch on to; I need illustrations and gimmicks and structures and frameworks that enable me to apply truth to my life.

God knows me well, so when He began to show me how critical it is to think correctly, He gave me a framework that I've used consistently for many years now. It is a simple approach to a profound doctrine and discipline. Any believer can understand it and practice it if she or he so desires, regardless of age, education, Bible knowledge, or intelligence. The results are far reaching and life changing. The method is easy to understand and simple—though not always easy—to apply.

Thinking That Is Narrow-minded

While the world tells us to be open-minded, God's Word teaches us a narrow way of thinking. We are to bring our thoughts into captivity—put them in a certain restricted area and keep them there!

If that sounds legalistic and confining, let me remind you that God's ways are not our ways. To realize the life-changing truth of biblical thinking, we must be willing to accept His ways. In reality I can assure you that this principle is not some great burden we must somehow learn to bear. Rather, by bringing our thoughts into captivity, we find great freedom. Let me illustrate it this way.

Many of you have skated on a lovely frozen pond in wintertime. You know that sense of freedom that allows you to go anywhere you like on that frozen surface. You can glide and turn and jump as much as you like to the extent of your ability. You have great freedom.

But suppose you decide you want to skate farther than the pond extends. You don't want to be confined to the frozen surface and choose instead to skate past the pond and into the grass and bushes and trees that surround it. After all, the scenery looks beautiful out there, and why should you be limited to skating only on frozen surfaces? So, you take off for the lands beyond the pond, feeling certain that since you're a good skater, you can navigate beyond the frozen surface.

Well, you'll find it a little difficult, won't you? Once you leave the frozen surface, your skates will bog down and you'll be stuck, going nowhere, no longer able to skate. You will lose all the freedom you had on that pond. So, in order to have the freedom you desire, you decide to stay within the boundaries of the frozen pond, knowing that any other decision is foolhardy.

Simple illustration, but do you get the picture? God has set boundaries for our thinking, and within those boundaries we have tremendous freedom. Those boundaries offer us all the area we need in which to move and think and grow and live. Within those boundaries we have plenty of room for individuality and creativity, for exploration and discovery, for new ideas and originality. But if we insist on exceeding those boundaries, instead of gaining more freedom, we'll only lose the freedom we have and get ourselves totally bogged down.

I have found this frozen pond image to be a helpful reminder for me. Often I'll say or think to myself, *Mary, you just skated off the ice and you're stuck in the mud.* Or, *Mary, you're headed for the bushes; stay on the frozen surface.* (I told you I was simpleminded.) This image has become a handy mental tool to bring every thought into captivity. I'll be using the pond illustration throughout the book in the hope that it will be equally helpful to you.

Thinking That Has Clear Guidelines

The next logical question we need to answer is: What are those guidelines? What are the boundaries? The Bible, of course, gives us the answers, and I believe these questions are most clearly answered in Philippians 4:8:

> Finally, brothers, whatever is true, whatever is noble, whatever is right, whatever is pure, whatever is lovely, whatever is admirable—if anything is excellent or praiseworthy—think about such things.

These words define the clear parameters of our thoughts and give us the secret to controlling our thought life. These words represent the boundaries of our "ice pond," so to speak. So, picture in your mind an ice pond with these boundaries.

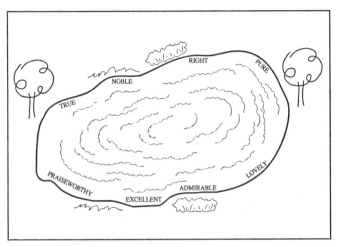

As long as our thinking fits within these parameters, we have freedom! Sounds like a contradiction, but it is truth. Frequently God's truth is paradoxical. If we want to be first, we have to be last; if we want to live, we have to die to ourselves; if we want to be a leader, we must be a servant. And here the Word of God gives us another paradox on which to build our lives: if we want to be free, we must think within the boundaries God has erected.

Thinking That Produces Right Living

Someone has said, "You can't think wrong and do right, and you can't think right and do wrong." It's a simple maxim that sums the matter up rather well.

Paul wrote to the Galatians: "But the fruit of the Spirit is love, joy, peace, patience, kindness, goodness, faithfulness, gentleness and self-control. Against such things there is no law" (Gal. 5:22-23). This is our biblical measuring stick to determine how closely our lives are controlled by the Spirit of God Who indwells us.

I wonder if that list leaves you a little breathless and perhaps discouraged, as it does me at times. Is the apostle serious? Am I truly expected to live my everyday life in such a way that I continually and consistently demonstrate love, joy, peace, patience, kindness, goodness, faithfulness, gentleness, and self-control? Doesn't he understand that my days are often filled with worries and problems, stacked with deadlines and workloads, surrounded with difficult people and strained relationships, and swamped in failure and defeat? Mission impossible, dear apostle—you just don't understand modern times. Your world must have been much easier than mine!

Not true, of course. Paul faced far more difficult situations and people than I'll ever encounter. And yet he seriously admonishes us, inspired by God's Holy Spirit, to live this kind of Spirit-filled life, producing the fruits that come from such a life.

Jesus said that we recognize plants and trees by the fruit they bear, and in the same way, we recognize people by the fruit they bear. Good trees produce good fruit; bad trees produce bad fruit (Matt. 7:15-18). And again He told us:

> I am the vine; you are the branches. If a man remains in me and I in him, he will bear much fruit; apart from me you can do nothing. . . . This is to my Father's glory, that you bear much fruit, showing yourselves to be my disciples.
>
> John 15:5, 8

Good thinking produces this good fruit. Good thinking comes from being attached to the Vine, Jesus Christ, and abiding in that Vine. Apart from that connection, we'll find it impossible to truly bring our thoughts in line with Philippians 4:8. We can't do it apart from Jesus Christ.

What does it mean to be attached to the Vine, Jesus Christ? It means you have consciously and deliberately made a decision to accept the salvation that He offers. That comes as a result of confessing your condition as a sinner, admitting your inability to do anything about your sin problem, recognizing that all the good works in the world will never qualify you to be attached to the Vine, and accepting the redemption that was purchased for you by Jesus when He died and rose again. When you take these steps, you become part of the body of Christ, and you are then a branch attached to the Vine.

If you do not know for certain that you've been attached as a branch, please resolve that issue at once. Contact your pastor or call my ministry office. Find someone who can clearly show you from God's Word exactly what it means to accept the salvation offered through Jesus Christ by faith. Knowing Christ as your personal Savior equips you with the ice skates that are essential for skating on the pond, so to speak. You'll get nowhere in this process without being attached to Him.

Assuming that most readers have made that decision, our challenge is not just to bear fruit, but to bear *much* fruit. The kind and amount of fruit we bear in our lives is directly related to and dependent upon how well we learn to think biblically, as described in Philippians 4:8.

Compare the fruit of the Spirit in Galatians 5:22-23 with our boundaries for right thinking in Philippians 4:8.

Boundaries for Thinking	Fruit of the Spirit
True, noble, right, pure, lovely, admirable, excellent, praiseworthy	Love, joy, peace, patience, kindness, goodness, faithfulness, gentleness, self-control

Is it not obvious that thinking within the Philippians boundaries will inevitably produce the fruit listed in Galatians 5? And the more we think according to Philippians 4:8, the more fruit we will bear in our lives.

There's the key to the Spirit-filled life that produces much fruit. It is not complicated; it is not mission impossible; it is not limited to only a few Christians. It is the *normal* Christian life as intended by our Heavenly Father when He gave us His Spirit to indwell us. It all begins in our minds, in our everyday thought processes.

Thinking That Brings Freedom

To the Romans Paul wrote:

Don't you know that when you offer yourselves to someone to obey him as slaves, you are slaves to the one whom you obey—whether you are slaves to sin, which leads to death, or to obedience, which leads to righteousness? But thanks be to God that, though you used to be slaves to sin, you wholeheartedly obeyed the form of teaching to which you were entrusted. You have been set free from sin and have become slaves to righteousness.

Rom. 6:16-18

With our obsession for personal freedom these days, we lose sight of the truth of this passage, that we are all slaves to whatever we obey. We choose to be either slaves to sin or slaves to righteousness. When we choose righteousness, we are set free from sin and its consequences.

The decision we face is whether we sacrifice the long-term for the short-term, whether we relinquish eternal benefits for temporary Band-Aids, whether we take the easy, wide road that leads to destruction or the narrow road that leads to life. The freedom that awaits us on this road to right thinking is the freedom from the consequences of wrong thinking—the consequences of sin.

For example, if and when I choose to obey these guidelines for biblical thinking, I will enjoy the freedom that comes from bringing my tongue under control. My relationships will improve; I'll be more effective on my job; I won't feel stress and guilt caused by inappropriate words. In short, I'll be free from all the consequences of a tongue out of control.

Conversely, if and when I choose not to obey these guidelines for right thinking, I will have to live with the consequences of a tongue out of control. I'll hurt people's feelings, intentionally and unintentionally; I'll damage my career with that loose tongue; I'll have lots of guilt as I remember things I've said that were inappropriate. I will lose the freedom that comes from right thinking, and I will have to live with the consequences of sin.

Do you remember the time when Peter was trying to give the Lord advice and Jesus strongly rebuked him? Jesus was trying to explain to His disciples that He had to go to Jerusalem and suffer at the hands of the religious leaders, and then be killed and on the third day be raised to life. Matthew tells us:

> Peter took him aside and began to rebuke him. "Never, Lord!" he said. "This shall never happen to you!" Jesus turned and said to Peter, "Out of my sight, Satan! You are a stumbling block to me; you do not have in mind the things of God, but the things of men."
>
> Matt. 16:22-23

Peter's problem here began in his mind. He had the wrong thoughts and that led him to wrong words and in so doing, he became a servant of Satan and a stumbling block to Jesus. That's a powerful statement from the Lord to Peter. It must have hurt his feelings deeply when Jesus accused him of being in allegiance with the Devil and told him he was a stumbling block. Surely that was not Peter's intention when he rebuked the Lord. I feel certain that he was not aware of his misguided and sinful thinking. He must have thought his response seemed so logical and right: Jesus should not die! But because his thoughts were contrary to God's thoughts, he became a tool of Satan and a stumbling block. He had to suffer the consequences of wrong thinking.

So, our first step on the road to right thinking, biblical thinking, is to agree with God's guidelines. We must accept God's boundaries and be in agreement with Him and His Word. Are you there? The fact that you've read this far in this book indicates a willingness on your part to get serious about biblical thinking. My guess is most of you would say, "Yes, I want to obey biblical guidelines for my thought life. I really want to know freedom from the consequences of wrong thinking."

Good! Now to the next step.

Thinking That Requires Awareness

In the last chapter we mentioned that the pursuit of right thinking is a spiritual battle. Let's look at 2 Corinthians 10:4-5 more closely:

The weapons we fight with are not the weapons of the world. On the contrary, they have divine power to demolish strongholds. We demolish arguments and every pretension that sets itself up against the knowledge of God, and we take captive every thought to make it obedient to Christ.

The *New American Standard* version says: "we are taking

every thought captive," and I prefer that small difference in the two translations.

Notice two things. First, *who* is to take our thoughts captive? We are! That's our job. Second, it is a continual process. "We *are taking* every thought captive," Paul wrote. It's not a once and for all undertaking; it is a lifelong pursuit. And third, every single thought must be brought into captivity.

This is a thought-by-thought process that requires daily attention and discipline. We must learn to listen to our thoughts and become very aware of them all the time. In fact, as we begin this journey together on the road to right thinking, I would encourage you to make such awareness your first assignment: Keep track of your thoughts very closely.

At the end of your day, make a few notes on how the day went. If it was a particularly good day, try to remember what your thoughts were during the day. Write down some of those specific thoughts, such as: *I thought about how beautiful the weather was. I thought about how glad I am that I have a good job. I thought about how blessed I am to have a good mate (daughter, son, etc.).* It will be very helpful if you identify your thoughts during a good day.

Obviously, the reverse is also true. If your day was lousy, remember the specific thought patterns you had during the day and note them. *I thought about what a jerk my boss is. I thought about how much my head hurts. I thought about how unfair it is that I have to _____* (fill in the blank).

Learn to listen to yourself think all through your day. When you feel angry, stop and identify what you're thinking. When you're fearful, make a note of exactly what path your thoughts are taking. When you feel peaceful, capture your thoughts. It's really a good idea to make some notes along the way, so that you will start to develop a strong awareness of your thoughts.

As I said in chapter 1, one of the main hindrances to right

thinking is that we don't think about what we think about; therefore, our thoughts wander around in whatever direction circumstances take them. If it's a good day, we have good thoughts. If not, we have bad ones. And we don't even realize what's happening to us because we don't think about what we think about!

At the end of this chapter I've given you a simple chart that you can use to keep track of your thoughts. I am convinced that if you've stayed with this book this far, you are serious about your thought life. But it could all fizzle at this point unless you start to become more and more aware of what you're thinking. So, please, force this bit of discipline into your life for a few days, and at the same time pray that God will give you more awareness of your thought patterns and habits so that you can determine when they are right and when they are wrong.

Preparing Your Mind

Peter wrote: "Therefore, prepare your minds for action; be self-controlled; set your hope fully on the grace to be given you when Jesus Christ is revealed" (1 Peter 1:13).

The *King James Version* translates this passage: ". . . gird up the loins of your mind . . ." Those are old-fashioned words, but they give us a graphic illustration of what it means to bring your thoughts into captivity.

"Girding up the loins" was a necessary action for men in Bible times when they wanted to run or move quickly. They wore those long garments that definitely got in the way when they were on the move. So they would grab those loosely flowing skirts, pull them up between their legs, fasten them to their belt or girdle, thus freeing themselves to run. Otherwise their own skirts would cause them to trip.

Preparing our minds is like girding up our skirts. We have to grab those loosely flowing, undisciplined, wandering thoughts and tie them up in order to have the freedom we need to run our race. Yes, it sounds contradictory, but it is nonetheless true. When we bring our thoughts into captivity, we are freed up to bear much fruit, to avoid the consequences of wrong thinking, to run the race that is set before us. But it takes mind preparation.

Are you ready? You have an exciting prospect in front of you. I invite you to dig into the next chapters, where we take an in-depth look into each of the boundaries mentioned in Philippians 4:8. Begin your journey down the road to right thinking.

Think About It

Here's a chart to help you think about what you're thinking about. You are welcome to copy this chart (and only this chart—don't forget the copyright laws!) to help you begin the needed discipline of becoming more and more aware of your thoughts. I've given you some sample entries to help you, but remember, you can devise your own method of record keeping if this doesn't suit you. The important thing is to begin practicing this discipline of thinking about what you're thinking about!

Date   Thought Pattern/Circumstances

Sample Entries:

Date	Thought Pattern/Circumstances
Monday	*I'm thinking about getting back at Shirley and telling her how thoughtless and cruel she is. She did it again—made fun of me in front of others at work. I thought about how my feelings were hurt.*
Tuesday	*I'm thinking about how tired I am—on and off all day long. I worked late last night getting laundry finished.*

Date	Thought Pattern/Circumstances

Chapter 3

THINKING WHAT

IS TRUE

My pastor once said, "We all have a right to our own opinions, but we don't have a right to our own truth." Well said. Have you noticed how many versions of truth there are today? Everyone seems to believe he or she has a right to a particular version of truth, and as a result we have a sliding scale of morality in our society that has fostered all kinds of trouble and tragedy.

For example, in the sixties we experienced what has been called the "sexual revolution," which proclaimed that sexual activity was a matter of choice. Society no longer accepted or taught the biblical absolute of sex only within the boundaries of marriage. "Whatever is right for you" became the guideline in most environments. Today we are reaping a horrific harvest that was sown by those seeds of untruth, with sexual diseases increasing and relationships breaking all around us, not to mention the spread of that ever-popular "low self-esteem," which we heap on ourselves when we adopt this untruth about sexual activity.

The lesson here is that when we believe things that are not true, then we base our actions on those untrue beliefs, and eventually we pay a very high price for those wrong beliefs. Truth by definition is unchanging and absolute. No matter how liberalized our society has become in substituting opinion for truth, people cannot change the truth about truth, no matter how loudly they proclaim their opinions or how fervently they believe them.

In 1982 there was a very sad episode in Chicago, where I then lived. Some deranged person put cyanide in Tylenol capsules randomly throughout the city, and as a result seven innocent people died. Mind you, when those seven people bought a bottle of Tylenol capsules, they believed it would cure their headache or stop their toothache or ease their backache. So the problem was not that these people doubted the helpfulness of this product; the problem was that they believed in a product that was, unknown to them, laced with death. The fact that they were unaware of the truth did not save them from death. Nothing could save them from the effects of that cyanide—not the sincerity of their beliefs, not the purity of their motives, and not even the innocence of their actions.

In a similar fashion, if we think about things that are not true, whether we believe they're true or not, we will suffer the consequences of that untrue thinking. Nothing can compensate for the lasting consequences of thinking things that are not true—not our sincerity, not our enthusiasm, not our naïveté, not our innocence, not our dedication, and not even our commitment. We must, therefore, learn to carefully scrutinize our thoughts for truth.

True Thinking

Something that is true is something that is in accordance with the facts. So when God's Word tells us to think about whatever is true (Phil. 4:8), our thoughts are to be factually correct. If there is any doubt about the validity of our facts, we should abandon the thought.

To begin to help you understand true thinking, try the following exercise. How would you classify the following thoughts?

True or Not True

___ *If my company does decide to lay some people off, I'm sure I'll be the first one to go! Then what will I do? I'll probably never find another job. And I'll go through my savings in no time!*

___ *I have a feeling that my boss will forget to give me that raise she promised me. I don't think she ever intended to give it to me anyway.*

___ *Andrea says she never sees Dave anymore. He always works late and never seems to have time for her or the family. I wonder if there's some extramarital thing going on? I can tell that Andrea is worried about what he's up to. After all, those are telltale signs of an affair.*

___ *I notice that Joan and Jim don't seem to be getting along very well lately. Maybe it's true what Patty told me, that they're considering a divorce.*

___ *My mother has never been pleased with me. Even as a child I could never do anything right. If I were more like my sister, I'm sure she would like me more.*

___ *My daughter is not doing well in school at all. She doesn't even seem to care. And her choice of friends is not good. It's all my fault because I haven't been the mother I should have been.*

___ *I'm afraid of what will happen if I take that new assignment. I'll probably do it wrong, and then my boss will be upset. I can imagine what he would do if I made a mistake on that account. He'd probably fire me.*

If we take a close look at each of these thought patterns, we'll discover that all of them are based on faulty speculations, unsubstantiated facts, false guilt, and/or unrealistic and unproductive imagining. You see, untrue thinking covers a broad spectrum.

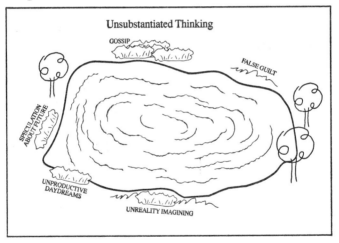

Lots of untrue bushes surround your mental ice pond—and mine—and they're often quite deceptive, appearing very innocent. We must be careful not to skate into these untrue bushes and get ourselves entangled in untrue thinking. So, let's take a closer look at some of these areas that can get us into great difficulty.

Speculations about the Future

Matthew 6:34 states: "Therefore do not worry about tomorrow, for tomorrow will worry about itself. Each day has enough trouble of its own."

I believe one of our most common excursions into untrue thinking is our tendency to speculate about what may or may not happen. These are the kinds of speculation that were illustrated in the first two scenarios earlier in this chapter.

If my company does decide to lay some people off, I'm sure I'll be the first one to go! Then what will I do? I'll probably never find another job. And I'll go through my savings in no time!

I have a feeling that my boss will forget to give me that raise she promised me. I don't think she ever intended to give it to me anyway.

These are examples of worrying about tomorrow, and Jesus explicitly told us not to do this. Yet I daresay that most of us indulge in this kind of untrue thinking much too frequently and easily. When we start speculating about the future, we almost always get ourselves into untruthful thinking.

When you look at it closely, worry is really just fear of the future, isn't it? We worry about what might or might not happen more than anything else. And we allow our minds to go into great detail imagining what the future holds. If you think about it, wouldn't you agree that about 90 percent of what we worry about in the future never comes to pass? And yet most of us indulge in worrying thoughts almost daily, without stopping to realize that we're allowing our thoughts to wander into territory God has forbidden.

Worry and trust cannot coexist. Any time we find ourselves

worrying, we know right away that we've stopped trusting God.

Now, strategizing for the future, setting goals, and making plans or contingencies is not the same as worrying about the future. Jesus told us to be shrewd as snakes (Matt. 10:16), and that would include thinking about how we should prepare for the future. God certainly doesn't intend for us to have an "I don't care what happens" attitude, and so, considering options and possibilities and making appropriate plans does not necessarily take us into untruthful thought patterns, unless we combine the planning process with worry and fear.

When we borrow trouble from tomorrow, worrying about what might or might not happen, speculating on the problems that might arise, our thoughts have left the boundary of "True." We have begun to indulge in improper thinking.

In Matthew 6:25-34, note what Jesus tells us specifically not to worry about:

• Do not worry about your life;
• Do not worry about what you will eat or drink;
• Do not worry about what you will wear;
• Do not worry about tomorrow.

Jesus gets right down to the basics, doesn't He? He knows us so well, and He understands how prone we are to worry about these things. In loving words He reminds us that we have a Heavenly Father Who knows our needs for tomorrow and is capable of taking care of those needs. And how kindly He tells us that our Heavenly Father will take care of our needs even though we have done nothing to earn His care.

Look at the birds of the air; they do not sow or reap or store away in barns, and yet your heavenly Father feeds them. . . . See how the lilies of the field grow. They do not labor or spin. Yet I tell you that not even

Solomon in all his splendor was dressed like one of these.

Matt. 6:26, 28-29

For me, this kind of future worrying is most evident when it comes to finances. With my controlling type of personality, I prefer to have a grip on the money issues. I want to know where the support for my ministry is coming from, to be assured that my personal income will adequately cover all my expenses, and to have enough money in the bank to cover any contingency.

In 1984 I began a radio ministry that is "listener-supported." (That's the term we use in Christian radio.) And I have trouble at times trusting those "listeners" to support our ministry adequately. I can find myself in the wee hours of the morning, lying in bed and worrying about what will happen if the funds we need do not come in. I have at times mentally gone through the process of shutting down the office, laying off staff members, selling all my possessions, and cashing in my retirement funds. This is exactly what Jesus was talking about when He said not to worry about your life, what you will eat or drink or wear, and not to worry about tomorrow.

When I worry about finances, I am engaging in untrue thinking because I am speculating about things that I do not know to be true—and in fact, have not yet come to pass. This untrue thinking produces worry, which is simply a lack of trust in God. That is sin at its worst. How could any of us not trust God Who has promised to take care of all our future needs? I may be somewhat justified in not trusting "listeners," but not trusting God is unjustifiable. He is totally trustworthy, and it is arrogant of us ever to doubt His promises to us. Worrying about the future is a slap in His face.

Of course, as a good steward of the ministry entrusted to

me, I must make adequate plans and take necessary steps to ensure that we are fiscally sound. The bills do have to be paid, and I cannot ignore my responsibility to think about and plan for future funding. But my challenge is to keep the line clearly drawn between the planning and administrative aspects of my position and my tendency to worry about money.

How often do you find yourself worrying about some of the things on that list that Jesus gave us? When you are anxious about any of these things, you've left the "true" boundary and you're entangled in the bushes I call "speculations about the future." Obviously, as long as you stay tangled up in those worry bushes, you are in bondage to them. Gone are your freedom of movement and your fun on the ice—all because you're thinking things that are not true.

Jeremiah 29:11 is a favorite verse for many of us: "'For I know the plans I have for you,' declares the Lord, 'plans to prosper you and not to harm you.'" If this verse is true, then how can we justify worrying about the future? And, taken in reverse, if we worry about the future, can we really say that we trust in God's good plans for us? Trusting God and worrying about the future are mutually exclusive—you can't do both.

If you find yourself worrying and speculating about your future, meditate and pray about this passage from Jeremiah and the one from Matthew 6. Ask God to help you truly understand how sinful it is to worry about these things, and ask Him to help you truly believe that He meant what He said when He promised to supply all of your needs.

Unsubstantiated Thinking

So often people tell me about the problems they have, particularly in their workplace, because of gossip and backbiting. It is truly malicious and harmful, and yet gossip is very common in most work environments and, unfortunately, in most other places as well, including our churches and our Christian community.

Gossip by definition is idle talk or rumors, and rumors are stories or statements without confirmation or certainty as to facts. How often do we allow our thoughts to dwell on unsubstantiated rumors that have not been confirmed by any facts? That's where gossip begins. If we never thought about rumors, we would never pass them along to others.

Think about the times during any given day when you are prone to think something about another person that you do not know to be factually true. Maybe your thoughts are similar to two of the examples at the beginning of this chapter.

Andrea says she never sees Dave anymore. He always works late and never seems to have time for her or the family. I wonder if there's some extramarital thing going on? I can tell that Andrea is worried about what he's up to. After all, those are telltale signs of an affair.

I notice that Joan and Jim don't seem to be getting along very well lately. Maybe it's true what Patty told me, that they're considering divorce.

Gossip begins with thoughts like:
Why didn't she call me back when she said she would? I wonder if . . .

He hasn't been at church lately. I really doubt his commitment . . .

Jim's been in the boss's office a lot this week. I bet they're finally fed up with . . .

She never speaks or smiles when she sees me. She thinks she's better than . . .

These are not true thoughts! They're not allowed.

The gossip bushes have thorns and briers as sharp as a knife, and the harm you inflict on yourself and others when you skate off the pond into the area marked "gossip" is long-lasting and painful.

Twice in Proverbs Solomon gives us the same warning about gossip: "The words of a gossip are like choice morsels; they go down to a man's inmost parts" (Prov. 18:8 and 26:22). Many times I've read those two particular proverbs and wondered exactly what Solomon was trying to say. Since he repeated himself, he must have felt this was an important principle about gossip that we need to understand. Having given it some thought, I believe Solomon was trying to emphasize that gossip causes long-term harm and pain that are difficult to expunge from a person's soul.

Perhaps if we could get some idea of the intense, long-lasting pain we foster when we gossip, the act of gossiping would start to become much more offensive to us. The Book of Proverbs lists some of the damages caused by gossip: a gossip betrays a confidence (Prov. 11:13a); a gossip separates close friends (Prov. 16:28b); and gossip causes quarrels (Prov. 26:20). Most of the time when we share rumors and gossip, or even when we listen to them, we are not thinking about the harm that can result.

Do you remember playing that gossip game when you were a kid? Someone started a rumor and passed it along through several other people. Finally, the last person to hear the rumor stated what he or she heard. Everyone laughed to see how the rumor had changed after being relayed several times. It was a fun game, but it was a game with a lesson attached about how gossip grows and how easily rumors become distorted as they are passed from one person to another.

And think about the far-reaching arm of gossip. If I tell you some gossip about a mutual friend or acquaintance, I can easily poison your mind against someone you previously held in esteem. By gossiping I transfer my opinions to you, influencing your thinking and causing you to see and relate to that person differently, even though you may never have had a negative experience of your own with that individual.

Why do you suppose gossip is so attractive to us? There's something about our old nature that jumps at the opportunity to hear some juicy story about someone. I must keep my antenna up all the time to beware of gossip. Some time ago I was with some Christian friends and the conversation gradually eroded into a gossip session. None of us intended it to happen, but we simply didn't have our guard up, and before long, we were saying things about others that were merely rumors. As the meeting broke up, I left with a heavy heart and a great conviction about how the conversation had drifted. I knew it was wrong, but I didn't have the nerve to try to direct the conversation in another way. Even though I didn't contribute to the rumors, I listened, and I listened with interest.

That wrong conversation took place because of wrong thinking. Had we refused to think thoughts of others that were unsubstantiated and unconfirmed, the words would never have formed on our lips.

Gossip begins in your mind and in mine. To win the battle against this malicious habit to which most of us are prone, we must get serious about cleaning up our thoughts and getting rid of gossip-filled thoughts. This is one area of right thinking that I am just now beginning to tackle seriously. Did you realize that in God's eyes thinking gossip is just as bad as saying it? And when I allow myself to think a bit of gossip, sooner or later I'm going to want to say it. So, the only way to ensure that I never gossip is to become very cautious about my thought life and not allow myself to think the gossip.

Paul wrote to the Ephesians: "Do not let any unwholesome talk come out of your mouths, but only what is helpful for building others up according to their needs, that it may benefit those who listen" (Eph. 4:29). This verse continues to convict and challenge me every time I read it. I have begun praying this verse into my life regularly, asking God to help me remember that nothing should come out of my mouth except what will build others up. Gossip always tears people down. It is never a benefit to those who listen; therefore, we should never speak even a one-sentence disparaging comment. But I can promise you, if you don't begin by cleaning up your gossip thoughts, you'll continue to indulge in gossip.

By the way, living by the principle of Ephesians 4:29 will cause you to be a quieter person. Most of us talk too much, and Solomon reminded us that where words are many, sin is not absent (Prov. 10:19). When we truly get serious about speaking only what will build others up, much of what comes into our minds and out of our mouths will cease. And that in turn will reduce our own stress and probably some of the stress we cause others through talking too much.

As I said, this is one area where I've dragged my feet in cleaning up my thought life. It just seems as though if I don't say those unkind, gossipy things I am thinking, then I'm innocent of gossip. But I've been learning that I have to dig deeper and get the thoughts of gossip out of my mind. Recently I was thinking about someone in an unwholesome way, and the Spirit of God convicted me about my thoughts. I realized again that if I refused to think unwholesome thoughts about others, I would never have to worry about saying them. If I make it my purpose in life to think about others in positive ways, in terms of building them up and benefiting them, I can be certain that my tongue will never utter gossip or anything unwholesome.

So, my first assignment is to clean out my thoughts and to recognize that it's just as bad to think unwholesome, gossipy thoughts as it is to say them. Furthermore, if I think them, I will eventually say them. It will happen!

False Guilt Thinking

One of our Enemy's favorite tools that he uses against us very effectively is false guilt. And often we are ever so good at assisting him in dumping all kinds of untruthful thoughts on ourselves—false guilt. Consider two of the examples at the beginning of this chapter.

My mother has never been pleased with me. Even as a child I could never do anything right. If I were more like my sister, I'm sure she would like me more.

My daughter is not doing well in school at all. She doesn't even seem to care. And her choice of friends is not good. It's all my fault because I haven't been the mother I should have been.

False guilt is that vague, awful feeling of inadequacy we dump on ourselves or allow someone else to dump on us. It is identified by its lack of specifics. When you feel guilty but you don't know exactly why or specifically what to do about it, that is almost always false guilt. False guilt feels just like true guilt, but there is quite a difference.

You see, true guilt is what we feel when we are under some conviction from God because we have chosen not to obey. God doesn't want us to feel guilty; He wants us to obey and get rid of the guilt. But when we choose to disobey, we are guilty and we feel guilty. To get rid of true guilt, we confess our sin and obey God. It is not confusing or complicated. The longer we put it off, the harder it becomes to do, but we are not in doubt about the cause or the cure for that true guilt.

False guilt, on the other hand, is what we feel when we allow ourselves to be condemned. Romans 8:1 gives us the wonderful truth that when we are in Christ, we are no longer condemned. Yet many of us live under condemnation, feeling guilty for things we have no right to feel guilty about, berating ourselves for things over which we have no control.

When we allow ourselves to think thoughts of condemnation, we have fallen into the Enemy's trap, and we are in for some depressing and discouraging days. You see, false guilt keeps us focused on ourselves, and any time we are self-focused, we are miserable.

Have you been trying to skate in the bog of condemnation? It is a terrible place to be. If you will start to keep thoughts of condemnation out of your mind, you will be able to rise above that lowland, you will start caring about other people and reaching out to them, and you will know the joy of living without condemnation.

I remember a period in my life when I allowed a person to condemn me. It took me quite a long time to recognize what was happening, but every time I was in her presence, which was frequently, I felt totally inadequate. I sensed that I never lived up to her expectations, and I tried very hard to be what she wanted me to be—even though I never knew exactly what that was. In my mind I was continually feeling that false guilt and trying to figure out what I should be doing, never knowing specifically what she disliked about me. I even asked her on several occasions, but she could not or would not specify any particular thing and indeed denied that there was a problem. But believe me, her condemnation was thick enough to cut with a knife sometimes.

The harder I tried to please her, the more she seemed to lay condemnation on me. I lived under this cloud of condemnation for quite awhile until God graciously revealed to me that I was allowing her to condemn me. When I finally saw this, I realized I could choose not to allow her to condemn me, regardless of her actions or attitude. She could only condemn me when I allowed it to happen because, of course, that condemnation was taking place in my mind, in my thoughts.

Once I began to refuse to let her condemn me, it was as though I had been set free from a terrible burden. She had no right to condemn; only Jesus has that right and He has promised me that He never will condemn me. So, I was set free from her condemnation. My mind was no longer plagued with those feelings of false guilt.

If your thoughts are frequently deluged with feelings of condemnation and you've been trying to skate in that muddy mess, I encourage you to take strong action to free yourself from that false guilt. It is all in your mind, don't forget. Once you get rid of the untrue thoughts, the false guilt has to leave. It has no place to reside when you put it out of your mind. You'll be back on solid ice, knowing freedom of movement and fulfillment of purpose in your life.

Unrealistic, Unproductive, and/or Unedifying Imagining or Daydreaming

Imagining and dreaming can be either helpful or harmful thinking. In Acts 2:17 we read:

"In the last days," God says, "I will pour out my Spirit on all people. Your sons and daughters will prophesy, your young men will see visions, your old men will dream dreams."

As this verse implies, dreaming and having visions are

things that can be a direct result of God's Spirit indwelling us. We need to have the ability to see what God wants to do through us and to dream about the possibilities and opportunities we have. So, there's no doubt that it is very possible to use our imaginations for good, for visions and inspiration, for motivational purposes.

But it is also possible for our imaginations to be out of control. For example, excessive indulgence in dreaming can lead you into an untruthful thought life that becomes an escape mechanism. How much time do you spend thinking about how you wish things were, dreaming of your ideal person or ideal set of circumstances, creating an unrealistic world of your own? When daydreaming becomes a daily or regular habit, it is unproductive and can be harmful. It is certainly not truthful thinking.

I'm not trying to lay guilt trips on you for innocent, normal daydreaming. But I know that my daydreaming can get out of control. Not too long ago I found myself indulging in a daydream for several days and allowing myself to build a fantasy of sorts, based on this daydream. It was a pleasant daydream, and I enjoyed imagining conversations, situations, etc. There was nothing wrong with the daydream itself—nothing immoral or unacceptable, but it began to take a great deal of my thought time. It became an escape.

When I began to realize that this daydream had gotten out of control, I didn't really want to abandon it. It was pleasant. Finally, I had to start forcing myself to abandon the daydream. I truly had to make a strong effort to keep myself from wasting valuable thought time on such a whimsical daydream.

It is amazing how our enemy can use such innocent things to try to make us ineffective. If he can't get us to think wrongly, he can absorb our thought life with unproductive fantasies. Daydreaming can be an escape mechanism, which used in moderation and in brief moments can be helpful. But how easily it can become a crutch for us to escape reality. We need to watch our daydreams and our imagination so that they do not push our thoughts outside the boundaries of our reshaped mind.

Consider the situation posed at the beginning of this chapter:

I'm afraid of what will happen if I take that new assignment. I'll probably do it wrong, and then my boss will be upset. I can imagine what he would do if I made a mistake on that account. He'd probably fire me.

This is an example of unproductive and unedifying imagining. Indeed these kinds of thoughts can turn out to be *self-fulling prophesies*. When we imagine what might happen, we usually imagine the worst, not the best. And then we set ourselves up for failure or prevent ourselves from pursuing goals and assignments that we should pursue for fear of failure.

Thinking Truthfully

Think about what is true. That simple five-word sentence encompasses a wide variety of thoughts. If this were the only guideline Paul gave us in Philippians 4:8, we would still see a tremendous change in our thought life by practicing true thinking.

Psalm 26:2 says: "Test me, O Lord, and try me, examine my heart and my mind." Ask the Lord to examine your heart and mind and to make you more aware of the areas in which you have difficulty thinking truthfully.

Think About It

When it comes to thinking what is true, which areas of your thought life seem to give you the most difficulty? Try to prioritize them by difficulty, with number one being the most difficult to control.

I worry about the future.
I indulge in nonproductive daydreaming.
My imaginings are out of control.
I think "gossipy" thoughts about others.
I allow others to condemn me.
I condemn myself.
I lay false guilt on myself.

If you're like me, you can only think of one thing at a time. So I encourage you to take the untrue thought pattern you identified as number one on that list above—the one that gives you the most difficulty—and spend one week asking God to help you work on that area specifically (refer to the prayer at the end of the next section). This will help you take specific actions to bring those untrue thoughts into captivity and get out of the bushes and back on the ice!

After you have worked for a few days on one specific untrue thought pattern, you can begin to work on other areas of untrue thinking if more than one gives you trouble.

Think about What Is True!

My greatest difficulty in thinking what is true is:

The last time I can remember thinking these kinds of untrue thoughts was:

I will pray this prayer (or one like this) every day this week.

Lord,

You know that I have difficulty thinking truthfully sometimes, and specifically I find that I indulge in (specify your number one area). Today would You please make me aware of every time I start to think like this? And then would You please give me the power to abandon that wrong thinking and get out of these untrue bushes?

Test me, O Lord, and try me, examine my heart and my mind.

Psalm 26:2

I give you permission to test my thoughts and mind, examine them closely and reveal to me when my thoughts are not true. I pray this in the powerful name of Jesus Christ, my Lord.

Amen.

Chapter 4

THINKING WHAT

IS NOBLE

Truth may not be noble. There is much truth in our world today that would never meet the noble criteria of being honorable, dignified, or excellent. Nobility goes beyond the black-and-white guidelines of accuracy of facts and takes us into the territory of motive and attitude.

For example, a person I know once said some untrue and unkind things about me and my ministry to at least three people and likely to many more. She intentionally sought to do me harm. I've had some difficulty with my thoughts about her. It is easy for me to think of the wrong she has done me and imagine all the things I'd like to say to her in response. My thoughts easily migrate into vengefulness and bitterness. I imagine how I could embarrass her or humiliate her by exposing her behavior and letting her know that I know what she's done. I have even hoped for bad things to happen to her because of how she's treated me.

Now, in this case my thought patterns were true. I had my facts straight. She had done the deeds that I was thinking of. But my thoughts were definitely not noble. To indulge in thoughts of retribution is definitely not noble thinking; therefore, according to Philippians 4:8, I should not allow myself to think those thoughts about her.

Let's take a closer look at some specific areas where our thoughts can easily entice us to skate off the pond and into "not noble" territory.

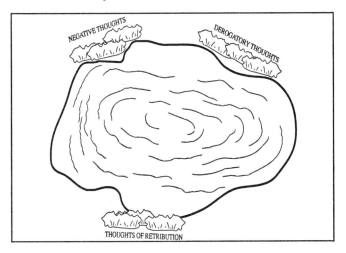

Focusing on Negatives Instead of Positives

I once worked for a man I described as my impossible boss. After a few months on his staff, I began to think of him in totally negative terms. He was intimidating and humiliating, he was arrogant and controlling, and he was not very nice to me. So, each day as I drove to work I focused on how difficult he was and how unpleasant it was for me to work for him. By the time I reached my office, I was fully prepared for a miserable day working for a "miserable man."

One thing you'll notice when you allow yourself to wallow in negative thought patterns is that your mind will inevitably magnify the negatives until they are blown totally out of proportion to reality. In retrospect I can see how I allowed this to happen in regard to this difficult boss. I thought so much about his negative characteristics that I made them much larger in my mind than they truly were.

After a few months I decided the obvious solution for this miserable problem was to find another job. I tried. Some sure-fire opportunities fell through, and after a year in this position, it began to dawn on me that I might be there for some time and my current mode of coping with my manager was disastrous. My performance was below par, my attitude was rotten, my testimony had been damaged, and my stress level was climbing every day. I finally realized that I had to make some changes in the way I thought about this difficult boss.

You see, in spite of the fact that he was not a good people manager, he was a very smart man. He had not attained his position without good reasons, and he had been successful because he was a very smart marketing man with lots of good ideas.

So, I made a conscious decision to reframe him and think about his good points instead of focusing on his bad ones. I took him out of the "Difficult Boss" frame and put him in the "Smart" frame. What a difference that made! I spent two more years in that job learning a great deal from that "impossible boss."

In reality I began to practice this part of Philippians 4:8— thinking about whatever is noble. And as soon as I changed my way of thinking, the relationship improved greatly, my performance improved, the job took on some added interest and challenge for me, and going to work was no longer a painful daily duty. In addition, I was able to be a much better witness for the Lord and have some positive impact in the lives of some of my coworkers.

I'm convinced that if I had not changed my thought patterns, I would probably have been fired for poor performance (and probably should have been fired), or at best spent two more miserable years in a job I hated. Instead, I gained valuable knowledge and experience that has proved very helpful in establishing myself as a self-employed business trainer. That has, in turn, allowed me to devote much of my time to the ministry the Lord has given me. So, that impossible boss was all a part of God's plan for my life. I sometimes wonder what would have happened if I had not changed my thinking. Maybe I wouldn't have been available and ready for the ministry that I have been so privileged to start and that I love very much.

Isn't it interesting how easily we remember the negative things we know about people but fail to think about their good points? We have those negative images sitting in our memory banks ready for instant recall. This is not noble thinking.

Ask yourself if you need to reframe someone or some situation in your life. It could be your mate or your children, your boss or your coworker, your pastor or your friend, your job or your location, your size or your personality. In many areas of our lives we can become so focused on the negative that we totally miss the positive. For example, when you look in a mirror do you see only the negatives about your looks? When you talk about your children, do you concentrate on what they should be rather than who they are? Do you constantly keep trying to make your mate the way you want him or her to be rather than appreciating what you have?

All of these things fall into the category of wrong thinking—perhaps true thinking, but never noble. Maybe you've justified your attitude because you are right. Your mate isn't perfect; your children have problems; your job is difficult; you are two sizes bigger than you should be! All true but all negative. You may need to do some constructive thinking about how to help your spouse or your children, or about how to improve certain situations, but simply magnifying the negatives without remembering the positives is wrong thinking. It will do you and your relationships much damage.

I've noticed how easily some people have become so focused on the negatives of their past that their present lives are dominated by the pain and suffering of days gone by. Certainly there are abundant examples of people who have endured great harm in their past, and I would never suggest that these experiences are inconsequential or that they can or should be dismissed with ease. Sin always produces consequences, and often innocent people suffer the consequences of someone else's sin.

In trying to find healing for past suffering, however, many have been led to focus so much on the harm done to them that their minds have become consumed with it, to their own detriment. Many times the pain is continued and elongated because they have been encouraged to think about the past, relive the past, place blame for the past, and so forth.

I remember talking with a woman who had had such a painful past and had struggled with the pain of that past for many years. In fact, she had become so focused on the harm done to her that she had little time or energy left for her husband and children. She almost lost her family because of her obsession with her past.

Finally, she began to spend significant time reading and studying the Bible, and gradually she refocused her thinking from her past to God's truth. She weaned herself from the earthly counsel that had led her to focus so much thinking on her past, and she learned the truth of Psalm 119:24: "Your statues are my delight; they are my counselors."

This woman found the healing she wanted by refocusing her thinking from the negatives of her past—true though they were—to the positives of God's goodness and love for her. She said to me, "Mary, I finally realized that I had to choose what I magnified in my life. Either I could magnify the pain of my past, or I could magnify the Lord. I have chosen to magnify the Lord in my mind, and that choice has enabled me to get beyond my past so that I now have a future and a hope."

Derogatory Thinking

Derogatory terms are never noble. How carelessly we think in these negative terms at times: the "jerk" in the car ahead of you; the "idiot" who parked his car crooked and took up two spaces; the clerks in the store who are "brain-dead;" the "dumb" people in the shipping department who get things mixed up. Often we employ this type of thinking about people we don't know.

It is very easy for me to think derogatory thoughts about nameless people. Because I teach customer service skills to business people, I am very aware of what is good customer service and what isn't. That in turn creates within me a very critical attitude toward people when I am the customer and they are supposed to be helping me.

I remember checking into a hotel one evening and the registration clerk did not give me the kind of service I expected. She was less than efficient, wasted my time, and broke several of my cardinal rules concerning good customer service. As I stood there waiting to finally get my room key, my mind was filled with all kinds of derogatory thoughts about her and her skills. Mind you, they were true thoughts, but they were far from noble.

Though I didn't say anything inappropriate to her, my body language and facial expressions certainly conveyed my lack of satisfaction with her behavior, and in the end she became aware of my thoughts. (You see, we can and do communicate our thoughts without saying a word!) I knew I had gotten my message across to her, and as I walked away to the elevator to go to my room, I felt very smug about how I had let her know that she did not perform properly.

As I stood waiting for the elevator, the Spirit of God spoke so loudly to me that I could not imagine why everyone else around me didn't hear the voice! Here's what God said to me at that moment: "You had one opportunity to show her what I am like, and instead you showed her what you are like." Zap! I'll never forget that moment for it is a lesson I have to relearn so often. I can so easily think derogatorily about people I don't know, and that can cause me to behave in unkind and unloving ways.

The only long-term solution for me is to work at changing my bad habit of derogatory thinking, and I am working on it. As soon as a derogatory thought enters my mind, I try to remember to refocus and think something like, "God loves that person just as much as He loves you." When I am successful at thinking nobly and getting rid of the derogatory thoughts, then I am able to respond in a Christlike way and show that person a little bit of what Jesus is like, instead of demonstrating what I'm like.

Have you noticed how easy it is to think derogatory thoughts about those in authority over you? These are people who have strong influences in our lives, so we think about them a good deal. Solomon warned us about this: "Do not revile the king even in your thoughts, or curse the rich in your bedroom, because a bird of the air may carry your words, and a bird on the wing may report what you say" (Ecc. 10:20). Notice what Solomon implies here: what we think becomes what we say. Your words begin with your thoughts, so don't even think thoughts about those in authority that you would not want to get back to them. We need to be careful how we think about our bosses, our pastors, our president, governors, mayors, etc. Your derogatory comments about a person will never get back to that person if you refuse to let yourself *think* the derogatory thoughts in the first place.

Have you ever indulged in these types of derogatory thoughts: *I think she looks dumpy in that dress. Can't imagine why she'd choose that style. Just makes her look heavier. And has she ever put on weight lately!*

Come on—admit it! You've been there and done that.

There's an old country story my father used to tell me about the man in town who always had something nice to say about everybody. It started to get to his friend, and one day the town drunk walked by. So his friend decided to confront him.

"Now, just tell me one good thing about that guy. He's always drunk, never does anything worthwhile, causes his friends and family a lot of trouble. What can you say good about him?"

His friend thought a minute and then replied, "Well, he sure can whistle good."

That's a phrase that has stuck in my mind all my life, and it is one I use to remind myself that I can always find something good to think and say about somebody if I want to.

We should not allow ourselves to think derogatorily about anyone, regardless of that person's behavior. It is not noble thinking. Noble thinking will cause us to dislike and discard those oh-too-easy derogatory thoughts.

Retributive Thinking

Do you have a strong sense of fair play? I do and some-times I think it is a curse because I can't stand to see people get away with something. I've often thought that if God had not redeemed me and given me new life in Christ, I'd be an angry, militant feminist, marching and fighting for my rights. My old sinful nature very much wants to get its "pound of flesh" and see people pay for their wrongdoing.

Thoughts of retribution, however, could never be classified as noble, regardless of whether that person deserves to suffer for his or her actions. Paul reminds us: "Do not take revenge, my friends, but leave room for God's wrath, for it is written: 'It is mine to avenge; I will repay,' says the Lord" (Rom. 12:19).

When someone treats you in unhelpful, unkind, or harm-ful ways, it's easy to justify a wrong response on your part. After all, that person doesn't deserve better! But think what you do when you allow someone else's poor performance to cause you to perform poorly. You allow that person to bring you down to his or her level because you've allowed yourself to think about retribution and revenge.

Here's another way to think about retributive thinking: don't wrestle with the pigs because when you do, you'll both get dirty, and the pig loves it! Just because someone else is not behaving properly, don't use that as an excuse to lower your standards and "wrestle with the pigs." Nobody wins when you and I do that. And remember, wrestling with the pigs begins in our thoughts. If we refuse to think in retributive, ignoble ways, we won't act in spitefulness or lower ourselves to the pigs' lev-els.

Also, keep in mind that if you insist on getting revenge, you won't leave room for God's wrath, and His method of avenging wrongdoing is much more effective than yours. So, don't get in God's way by insisting on having your revenge. That person may be off your hook, but he or she is not off God's hook. So, refuse those thoughts of retribution and let God do the avenging.

Distinguishing between Awareness of Wrong and Wrong Thinking

You may find yourself in a bit of a dilemma as you try to determine what is noble thinking and what is not. Does noble thinking mean we ignore the bad things we recognize in others? How can we have a righteous sense of sin and evil and still think nobly about people who are sinful and evil? How can we think of others' positives and not their negatives? Should we think only of their positives? Isn't that sticking our heads in the sand and living in denial?

These are not easy questions. Let's look at two examples of how our Lord reacted to sinful behavior.

> Jesus entered the temple area and drove out all who were buying and selling there. He overturned the tables of the money changers and the benches of those selling doves. "It is written," he said to them, "'My house will be called a house of prayer,' but you are making it a 'den of robbers.'"
>
> Matt. 21:12-13

> The teachers of the law and the Pharisees brought in a woman caught in adultery. They made her stand before the group and said to Jesus, "Teacher, this woman was caught in the act of adultery. In the Law Moses commanded us to stone such women. Now what do you say?" They were using this question as a trap, in order

to have a basis for accusing him.

But Jesus bent down and started to write on the ground with his finger. When they kept on questioning him, he straightened up and said to them, "If any one of you is without sin, let him be the first to throw a stone at her." Again he stooped down and wrote on the ground.

At this, those who heard began to go away one at a time, the older ones first, until only Jesus was left, with the woman still standing there. Jesus straightened up and asked her, "Woman, where are they? Has no one condemned you?"

"No one, sir," she said.

"Then neither do I condemn you," Jesus declared. "Go now and leave your life of sin."

John 8:3-11

In the first case, Jesus was dramatic, forceful, angry, and "in their face" about degrading His Father's temple. He offered no counseling session, no compromise. Rather, He abruptly confronted the money changers and threw them out. He made no pretense of sparing their feelings or trying to salvage their dignity.

In the second situation, Jesus seemed to have a world of patience with the woman caught in adultery. Notice that the Pharisees said the Law commanded that the woman be stoned. In Leviticus 20:10 we see exactly what the law said: "If a man commits adultery with another man's wife—with the wife of his neighbor—both the adulterer and the adulteress must be put to death." Jesus would not be fooled by the Pharisees' pretense at righteousness, and He saw through their attempt to trap Him. Furthermore, He refused to condemn this woman. When He was alone with her, He quietly addressed her problem: "Go now and leave your life of sin." He did not condone her sin, but He dealt with her very nobly, with dignity and honor.

What do you think made the difference in Jesus' outward reaction to the sin He recognized in these two situations? I believe Jesus' reactions were different because He knew the hearts and motives of the sinners involved. The money changers were more than aware that what they were doing was wrong. They knew the law and regulations regarding the temple, yet because of greed they chose to defile God's temple. They were charging exorbitant prices and deceiving the people who came to worship and offer sacrifices. They were exploiting this most holy of duties, prescribed by the Law of Moses, for dishonest profit. Jesus would have none of it. The money changers were also harming others and leading them astray in the worship of the true God. Their actions were blasphemous and dangerous.

In the adulterous situation, Jesus knew the hearts of the Pharisees and saw through their hypocrisy. They were accusing this woman while their own hearts were heavy with guilt. We don't know what Jesus wrote on the ground, but undoubtedly the words shamed these men and caused them to run away like cowards. Notice that the older men were first to go. I've always wondered why, and furthermore I've wondered why John made it a point to tell us that detail. Perhaps their names were at the top of a list Jesus wrote on the ground. At any rate, the principle Jesus was teaching is clear: when dealing with someone else's sin or shortcoming or mistake, tread very softly and make certain that you first consider your own life. You are free to "throw stones" when you can honestly say you're not guilty of any wrong yourself. Who of us is in that place? (If you think you are, I'm afraid you've got a bigger problem called pride!)

Jesus, however, does not want us to be soft on sinful

behavior, and there will be times when the right thing to do is to take some strong action or speak strong words to denounce sin. This requires a great deal of prayer and discernment to be sure that this kind of response is from God and not simply driven by our need for revenge. We would do well to follow Jesus' example: when He was personally mistreated by someone behaving sinfully, He did not respond or stand up for Himself, but when He observed someone acting sinfully and doing harm to others, Jesus was forceful.

Matthew gives us another insight into how Jesus responded to those who were sinners:

> As Jesus went on from there, he saw a man named Matthew sitting at the tax collector's booth. "Follow me," he told him, and Matthew got up and followed him.
>
> While Jesus was having dinner at Matthew's house, many tax collectors and "sinners" came and ate with him and his disciples. When the Pharisees saw this, they asked His disciples, "Why does your teacher eat with tax collectors and 'sinners'?" On hearing this, Jesus said, "It is not the healthy who need a doctor, but the sick."
>
> Matt.9:9-12

Here Jesus makes it clear that He has a loving and caring attitude toward people who are classified as "sinners." He came to deliver them from their sins, and He loves the sinner.

I think these examples of our Lord give us some very good guidance as to how we can think nobly about people, even if their actions aren't what they should be. These passages of Scripture also give us some insight on how clearly we need to take a stand against sinful acts and attitudes. But we need always to be careful to love the sinner.

The Challenge of Thinking Nobly

How can we develop a sense of righteousness and hatred of evil, as we should do, and still think nobly about people who are sinful? When I see behavior in others that is obviously not Christlike (particularly in other believers), I cannot ignore that behavior. The closer I walk with God, the more I will be aware of behavior and characteristics that are not honoring to God. How, then, do I keep from thinking negatively about these people?

Well, step number one is to pray for them immediately. Just pray for the particular problem that you see in their lives, and pray that God will reveal it to them so that their lives can become more Christlike. Then, remember that you may be guilty of the same offense or something worse, and remind yourself that you are not called to condemn others. At this point it is important to commit to the Lord that you will not talk about this thing to others.

That's what I've come to in my thinking about this woman who has spoken ill of me and my ministry. When I start to rehearse and rehash the wrong she has done, I force myself to stop and pray that she will see the error of her way and repent. I've asked God to give me a heart of compassion for her, rather than a feeling of revenge toward her. I want to see her repent, not to justify me but for her own good, knowing that until she does, her fellowship with the Lord will be hindered. In fact, it is not even necessary for me to know if she has repented. She may do so—indeed, may have already done so—and I would not know it. That is not the important issue; the important issue is that she, as a fellow believer, would have a clear conscience toward God so she can be effective for His service.

I can assure you that thinking nobly about her did not come easily or naturally for me at first. Like everything else in the

Christian life, I had to do this by faith and not by feelings. So, disregarding my feelings, I acted on what I knew was right and continued to change my thinking and bring it into the realm of noble. There were some days I had a hard time doing that and those thoughts had to be tackled more than once during the day. But as I continued to change my thinking and pray for her, the feelings started to change and now it no longer even enters my mind on a daily basis. So, it is possible to make permanent changes in our thoughts by making ourselves think biblically.

It is always good to learn lessons from the negative things you observe in the lives of others, but do not dwell on them. When you find yourself starting to think about those negatives again, just stop and pray for that person, and then put the negatives out of your mind. Try to find something nice about the person on which you can concentrate, or at least start thinking of something or someone else.

I want to be aware of unrighteousness, in myself and in others, but I don't want to have a critical and condemning spirit toward others. The solution is in how I think about people. I believe that praying for others immediately when I recognize wrong behavior will keep me from thinking wrongly—keep me from thinking thoughts that are not noble.

Think About It

Indicate which of the following ignoble thought patterns are areas of concern in your life:

__ I focus on the negatives, ignoring the positives.

__ I exaggerate the negatives in my mind.

__ I think of things I could do to get revenge.

__ I wish and hope for bad things to happen to someone.

__ I think of wrongs done to me many years ago.

__ I think critical and derogatory thoughts about others (i.e., their looks, behavior, personality, size, opinion, intelligence, etc.).

Other:

Ask yourself these questions:

Yes or No

__ Is there one particular person in my life toward whom I have thoughts of revenge or retribution?

__ Is there one specific event in my life that has created a lot of ignoble thinking?

__ Is there a particular category of people toward whom I am more prone to have derogatory thoughts? (For example, men or women, young or old people, people in certain jobs, a certain race of people, people with less or more education than I have, rich or poor people, family members.)

__ Do I often mentally criticize strangers who come across my path—their looks, their behavior, their intelligence, etc.?

Identify people you know whose actions/behavior/lifestyle are not appropriate, and indeed may be sinful or evil.

What can you do to avoid thinking wrongly about these people?

Pray for them regularly, that they will see their sin and be willing to change.

Think about their good, positive characteristics and traits.

Remember that God loves these people as much as He loves you!

What will you do and when will you begin?

I will   ## Beginning

_____   _____

_____   _____

_____   _____

_____   _____

_____   _____

_____   _____

_____   _____

_____   _____

Chapter 5

THINKING WHAT

IS RIGHT

S ome years ago a friend was helping me at a church function, and I noticed that she was somewhat abrupt and rude with some women of another race. Yet, in dealing with women of her own race, she was hospitable and kind. This bothered me greatly, and I struggled with how best to deal with the situation. Finally, I found a way to remove her from that position so she would not have direct contact with these women.

When I talked with her, she freely explained that she didn't trust these women of the other race because she had to work with this type of women on her job, and she found them to be dishonest and lazy. She felt they could not be trusted.

I was angry at her attitude; it was not right! In her mind she had allowed herself to follow what seemed to be a logical progression of thought, concluding that she had to beware of certain women of another race because, as a whole, women of that race were not to be trusted. It all began in her mind. Yet she would have vehemently denied being prejudiced and would simply have described her attitude as realistic.

In her case, the causes of this wrong thinking were some difficult experiences she had had on her job, combined with an attitude passed down to her by her parents and our society. Remember that much of our thinking is conditioned from our past so we must carefully examine our thoughts to uncover prejudices or biases that we've inherited.

According to Philippians 4:8 our thoughts are to be right—equitable and fair. That means that in our minds, every person we know, every stranger we meet, every group or nationality or race or gender should be on equal footing, on level ground. We should think the same way about people, regardless of their external characteristics or circumstances.

I've discovered that few people ever think of themselves as prejudiced. Rather, they have rationalized their prejudicial thinking and explained away their unfair attitudes. You can probably think of someone you know who is like this.

You and I must search our hearts deeply and ask some painful questions to discover if we are like this. Have we explained away our prejudice, filing it in some other mental category and believing ourselves to be justified for wrong attitudes?

Christians, of all people, should never be guilty of prejudice or discrimination. We should have reputations as individuals, and as bodies of believers, for treating people justly and fairly no matter who they are. Sadly, this is often not the case, and even within the body of Christ we see some shocking evidence of unfair, prejudicial, discriminatory attitudes. Our challenge, if we are to think rightly, is to dig up those roots of unfair and inequitable thinking that have become part of the landscape of our minds.

So, if your first reaction is that you could skip this chapter because you are not guilty of bigotry or prejudice, I beg you to keep reading. I have discovered that all of us have some cleaning up to do when it comes to right thinking.

Try to answer these questions honestly.

• Have you ever found yourself mentally accusing someone else without proof or evidence? Some money is missing from petty cash. Does your mind immediately go to a person on the job who has a reputation for dishonesty?

• Do you think prejudicially about people of other races, cultures, nationalities, the opposite sex? You're walking down the street and a man of another race, another color, is walking toward you. Do you cross the street?

• Have you allowed something in the past to prejudice your attitude toward some person or people in your present? Maybe your ex-husband was verbally abusive. Do you tend to classify men you know as abusive because they remind you of your ex-husband or simply because they are men?

Chances are, if you're honest, you will have to admit that not all of your thinking is right and fair.

Let's look at some of the prejudicial mud and mire that lurk on the edges of our mental ice ponds. You may be stuck in one of these without realizing it.

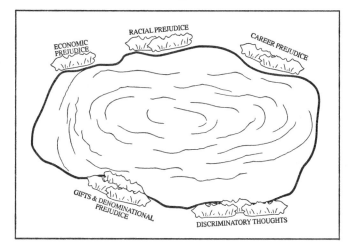

83

Racial Prejudice

The type of prejudice that comes to mind most readily is racial prejudice. In spite of years of legislation and efforts by many groups, racial prejudice has not disappeared in our society. In fact, some would say it is worse than ever. Legislation and social programs will never end racial prejudice. They may be necessary, but they are Band-Aids on a cancer. Prejudicial attitudes will change only when we change the way people think.

I am a middle-class, white woman. Though I may try to understand racial prejudice and never participate in it myself, because I am a white woman, I'll never be able to understand totally what it feels like to be treated prejudicially simply because of my skin color. But as a white, Christian woman, I still have a strong obligation to work hard at understanding and rooting out racial prejudice. I also must work hard at understanding and relating to people of other races, particularly my sisters and brothers in Christ.

The Apostle Peter had to learn about racial prejudice. As recorded in Acts 10, Cornelius, an Italian, wanted to know the true God, and Peter was commanded in a vision to share the truth about Jesus with him and his family. Peter didn't want to do that because he believed the Gospel was only for the Jews.

But in this vision he saw all kinds of animals and reptiles and birds, and a voice told him to kill and eat them. Peter refused because they were impure and unclean, but God said to him, "Do not call anything impure that God has made clean" (Acts 10:15). Through that vision God changed Peter's thinking about other races. Peter had to unlearn what he'd been taught by his parents, his religious leaders, his society, and his peers, and he had to think about other races in a totally different context.

Once he was made aware of his wrong thinking, Peter accepted right thinking—he was not to call anything impure that God had made clean. So Peter shared the Gospel with Cornelius and later he said, "I now realize how true it is that God does not show favoritism but accepts men from every nation who fear him and do what is right" (Acts 10:34-35). Peter began to face the wrong thinking that was within him, and he started to change it.

It's no accident that Jesus used a Samaritan in His parable about being a good neighbor. By telling a story about a kind Samaritan who helped a wounded Jew, Jesus clearly proclaimed that He harbored no prejudice toward the Samaritans. He saw them as equal and treated them with respect.

If racial prejudice has been instilled in you from your parents, school, culture, friends, or your own experience, it is critical that you face up to that wrong thinking and start a campaign to clean up your mind. If wrong thinking has been deeply imbedded, you may have to invest much time and effort to clean up your mind. Your thought life will never be "right" until you do it.

As believers, you and I can take some concrete, specific actions to get rid of the prejudice within ourselves and start to think rightly.

1. Cultivate friendships with people of other races. Invite a mixed group to your home for dinner. (Has anyone of another race ever been invited into your home?) These could be people from your church or your job or your neighborhood. Gather them in your home, cook a meal for them, and just get to know them in that intimate setting. And don't do it as a novelty; do it to begin a friendship that can continue.

I've formed some strong friendships with women of other races over the years, and so when I think about prejudice in our society toward people with different skin colors, I hurt for my friends. If your circle of friends has no variation in color, if all of your friends are of the same race as you, something's wrong. If you will make an effort to get to know believers of another color and/or race, you'll be amazed how those relationships will change your thinking and help you think what is right and fair. Any prejudices you hold will begin to die on the vine.

I remember one occasion when my Tanzanian friend, Gertrude, was visiting Chicago and I met her for dinner in a public place. We were so happy to see each other, and hugged as friends do, and with great enthusiasm as Africans do. I noticed some white people around us watching as though this were unusual or strange—two women of different colors obviously good and dear friends. But we are one in Jesus; we're going to be in heaven together. What's so strange about loving each other and expressing it openly?

Paul wrote to the Galatians: "You are all sons of God through faith in Christ Jesus, for all of you who were baptized into Christ have clothed yourselves with Christ. There is neither Jew nor Greek, slave nor free, male nor female, for you are all one in Christ Jesus" (Gal. 3:26-28).

2. If your church tends to be all white or all black or all of any particular race, find a way to have fellowship with believers of other races. Maybe invite some people of another race to your church or plan a meeting where you join together. Start a Bible study with a racial mixture to it. I promise you, one of the sweetest and best ways to change your thinking is to pray with and for fellow believers of other races and to listen to them pray for and with you.

Also, share their worship experience. It may be quite different from yours, but you can gain much from worshiping with them. I know that my spiritual life has been greatly enriched by worshiping with the wonderful cultural mixture that we have at The Christian Working Woman events. Because it is a radio program, our ministry seems to cross barriers and bring races together in a unique way. We have found such joy in sharing each other's music and worship styles. Worshiping and praising God together bonds you in a very special way, as does praying together.

As I write this chapter, I've just returned from a three-week missions trip to East Africa. We had many opportunities to be with Christian women in these countries, and I was deeply impressed with their depth of spirituality and commitment to Jesus Christ. Some of those women could pray circles around me! Their lives challenged me in my walk with Christ. I gained so much from fellowshiping with them. How sad when we miss the richness we have in the body of Christ because of prejudicial thinking. And how sad that racial prejudice still exists in the church.

3. Ask God to show you where you have prejudicial attitudes. Since it's very easy for us to reclassify prejudice and unfairness into other more acceptable categories, we may be quite unaware of the mental stereotyping that has become ingrained in our minds. David prayed, "Who can discern his errors? Forgive my hidden faults" (Psalm 19:12). Another translation says, "Show me my hidden errors." That is a good prayer for all of us when it comes to revealing attitudes in our minds that are not right and need to be changed.

I was saddened recently to hear of some older people in a very good church who still harbor stereotypical attitudes toward people of another race and blatantly express that prejudice. Of course, they don't see it as prejudice; it's just the way they have always thought, and they've never been able to see how sinful their attitudes are. These are godly people who serve God faithfully in many ways, but their thought lives are full of wrong thinking about this other race of people. Even sadder is the fact that in their later years, they are not likely to change their ways of thinking. A friend has tried to point out how unbiblical their attitudes are, but their minds have been so long set in this rigid prejudicial mindset, that her attempts have been unsuccessful.

You see, the longer you allow your mind to be filled with thoughts that are not right, that are prejudicial, the harder it is to see the error of your thinking and then change. But however old you are, or whatever stage you're in, you can know freedom from prejudicial thinking if you will pray and ask God to reveal these things to you and to give you the power to change your thinking.

4. *If you've never personally experienced racial prejudice, talk to Christians who have and ask them what it's like.* Let them share their pain with you so you can feel it. We are to carry each other's burdens and so fulfill the law of Christ (Gal. 6:2), and one way we do that is to feel the pain others feel because they've been treated prejudicially in our society.

Economic Prejudice

Of course, there are other prejudices within us that we need to face. A very common one is the prejudice we often have toward poor people or people with lesser means—an economic prejudice. In Job 34:19 we are reminded that God "shows no partiality to princes and does not favor the rich over the poor, for they are all the work of his hands."

James puts it even more graphically when he writes:

Suppose a man comes into your meeting wearing a gold ring and fine clothes, and a poor man in shabby clothes also comes in. If you show special attention to the man wearing fine clothes and say, "Here's a good

seat for you," but say to the poor man, "You stand
there," or, "Sit on the floor by my feet," have you not
discriminated among yourselves and become judges
with evil thoughts?

James 2:2-4

You know, we all tend to judge people by the way they're
dressed, by their accumulation of wealth or things, by the way
they walk or carry themselves. An interesting experiment is to
notice how you're treated when you go shopping dressed as a
professional versus shopping while wearing your casual jeans
or sweats. The clerks in the stores are just naturally prejudiced
against the sloppy look, and most of them give much more
attention to the customer who is well dressed. It's a tendency
we all have.

Notice that James says when we treat people differently
based on their economic status, we have become "judges with
evil thoughts." We are judging others, which, of course, is forbidden. Jesus said: "Do not judge, or you too will be judged"
(Matt. 7:1).

This evil judgmental attitude begins with our thoughts, as
we allow ourselves to think of people differently based on
their economic status, their wealth and what they have accu-
mulated in this world's goods.

Like other prejudices, we overcome these thoughts by
putting ourselves in the shoes of other people and getting to
know people who are different from us. When we live isolat-
ed lives and never associate with people from different economic strata, we will be much more prone to have distorted
and incorrect ideas and attitudes toward these people.

If your lifestyle keeps you separated from people who are
not like you, it would be most helpful to find ways to increase
your association and involvement with those people. Perhaps

a different church would give you that opportunity. Maybe you could locate a Bible study group with economic diversity or become involved in outreach programs to help underprivileged people.

A young woman in our church has started a Bible study group for women in a public housing complex located near our church. She is now bringing some of those women to our church functions for women and bringing their children to our Sunday School. They are lovely women, no different from the rest of us in their dreams and desires, their heartaches and struggles.

Knowledge and familiarity are keys to overcoming all kinds of prejudice, but we have to reach out and find ways to get to know each other.

Career Prejudice

Not long ago someone met me and told me of her career position and how successful she has been and asked if I could connect her with other Christian women equally successful. She said she found it difficult to relate to most workplace women since her position was at a much higher level than most women's. I thought, *That shouldn't be true. If someone is your sister in Christ, you should be able to relate. What difference does it make what job you have?*

A person who is a lawyer or a doctor or an accountant is likely to get more respect than a secretary or a file clerk or a janitor. I find that it is a continual exercise in mental control to respect and appreciate people based on who they are, not on what position they have.

On my recent missions trip to East Africa, I met a man and his wife, David and Esther, who work at Tinwet Hospital in Kenya. David is a native Kenyan who accepted Christ into his life as a teenager. His story of how God has directed his life and provided for him and his family is remarkable. As I sat in his humble home and listened to him tell us about what God has been doing through his ministry, I knew that I was in the presence of a spiritual giant. I felt humbled just to be with him and his wife. His heart burns with a passion to reach people for Jesus, and he works tirelessly, doing the jobs of three people because he loves Jesus so much. He leads thousands of people to Christ every year, in the hospital and in the surrounding churches that he oversees.

The more people I meet and know like David and Esther, the more I realize how foolish it is to evaluate people by earthly success or credentials. David's career credentials would probably not impress anyone greatly. He has not achieved a status that the world would recognize or honor. Yet his life is a rare testimony to God's power and grace. When we get to heaven those job titles and promotions are not going to count for anything. God will not be impressed with our career success.

Please don't ever say, "I'm *just* a secretary—or *just* a janitor—or *just* a homemaker—or *just* anything." You are contributing to your own prejudicial thinking concerning careers and earthly status. As long as we are doing what God has given us to do, we never have to apologize for our position.

When I started my radio ministry, I thought of different names for the program, such as Professional Christian Women or Christian Business Women, but I decided against them because I didn't want to give anyone the idea that what we classify as professional has any more significance to God than any other career. So, I named the ministry The Christian Working Woman, which puts all listeners on level ground. While we can respect and admire the work and accomplishments of others, it is biblically wrong to treat others better or worse or think of them differently based on their careers.

In Romans 12:16 we read: "Live in harmony with one another. Do not be proud, but be willing to associate with people of low position. Do not be conceited." That sums it up rather concisely. We have a direct command to associate with people whose positions may be on a lower rung of the ladder than our own position.

Gift and Denominational Prejudice

Did you ever think about the prejudice we have toward people's spiritual gifts?

We tend to think some gifts within the body of Christ are more important than others. Often, less visible gifts, such as hospitality, administration, and mercy get shortchanged. But all gifts are equally important and should be valued and appreciated equally.

I happen to have a gift that is visible—it puts me up in front of people. I often pray, "Lord, deliver me from the celebrity syndrome." That is my way of saying, "Remind me often that I'm a servant and that my gift is no more special than anyone else's."

Paul wrote to the Corinthians:

For who makes you different from anyone else? What do you have that you did not receive? And if you did receive it, why do you boast as though you did not?

1 Cor. 4:7

Regardless of the gifts we have or the amount of talent and ability we possess, we must continually remember it has been given to us as a gift to be used to glorify God. And to whom much is given, much will be required. So, rather than boasting of our gifts, we should be making certain that we are good stewards of what God has entrusted to us, for we will be held accountable for our use of the gifts we have.

Within the body of Christ we also often detect denominational or doctrinal prejudices. Certainly we need to know God's Word and stand strong and true on basic doctrines that can never be compromised. But dear friends, there are many areas where we can have differences of opinion and belief and still have sweet fellowship.

Do you think that your way is the only way to worship? Are you prejudiced toward people who do it differently? Do you think such people are less spiritual or outdated or too rigid or too emotional? Try visiting other kinds of Bible-believing churches and see how wonderful it is to worship God in a new way. I love the way African-Americans worship, with emotion and gusto and without regard to clocks. I love their music; it touches my heart.

I also love the classical, more liturgical type of worship. I've visited churches with strong ecclesiastical services and found great beauty and depth in the rituals when they are biblically based and doctrinally sound. The old hymns can hardly be replaced for meaning and splendor, and we should not overlook them just because we have some new ways of singing now.

Discriminatory Thinking

According to *Webster's,* discriminatory thinking is making a distinction in favor of or against a person on the basis of the group or class to which the person belongs, rather than according to merit.

Jesus made a point of ignoring the discriminatory thinking of His day and teaching His disciples to do the same. For example, when He chose to talk to the Samaritan woman at the well, He shocked the disciples because Jews hated Samaritans and considered all of them to be second-class citizens. Jews never talked to Samaritans unless they had to, and men never talked to women in public because women were considered inferior to men. So, according to the thinking of the day, this Samaritan woman had two strikes against her: she was a Samaritan and she was a woman. For both reasons the disciples would never have spoken to her at that well. Their thinking had been polluted by their culture, and they had accepted the prejudices handed down to them by their parents and leaders. But Jesus chose not only to talk to this Samaritan woman, but also to reveal great and marvelous truth to her, leading her to become His follower. Jesus did not allow discriminatory thinking to keep Him from seeing this woman for who she was—a person who needed salvation.

Think about the people you know. Do you see them as God sees them—thirsty for salvation?

Try asking yourself these questions:

- How do I treat people who aren't as smart as I am?
- How do I treat people who aren't as sophisticated as I am?
- How do I treat people who are more shy or timid than I?
- How do I treat people who are less educated than I am?
- How do I treat people who are less cultured than I am?
- How do I treat people who are older or younger than I am?

The list could go on and on. If one or two of these questions have pointed out to you that you think discriminatorily about a person you know, or a group of people you know, ask God to begin to help you make some changes in your thought life. It won't be easy, but it is necessary.

When we allow ourselves to be shaped by prejudice from our childhoods, environments, or experiences, we are not thinking rightly. Our thinking is unfair. We have stereotypes in our minds of other types of people—other races, other nationalities, other personalities—and we tend to fit everyone we meet into those unfair categorizations. I fear that this is a common malady among all of us, including Christians.

Ask God to help you dig up any prejudice that may have been rooted in your mind from childhood. As long as you allow yourself to think about people in a prejudicial way, you're going to be bogged down in the mud and the mire instead of skating on the frozen surface.

Think About It

Check any of the following statements that are true.

__ My parents have (or had) strong prejudicial attitudes toward another race or races.

__ I grew up in what would be considered by most as poverty.

__ I was raised in an affluent home.

__ When I meet people for the first time, I find it helpful to know their job titles.

__ I have worshiped the same way most of my life.

__ When I meet people for the first time, I find it helpful to put them in categories.

Now, look at that list again. Do your check marks represent any thinking that needs to be changed?

What actions could you take to change those prejudicial thought patterns that are not right?

__ I will spend some time thinking and praying about the prejudicial beliefs my parents held or still hold.

__ I want to enlarge my circle of friends to include other races.

__ I want to start or become a part of a racially mixed Bible study.

__ I will spend some time working with economically disadvantaged children/people.

__ I will make a conscious effort not to ask people what their job titles are when I am introduced to them.

__ One Sunday I will attend a church that worships differently than my church.

__ I will pray that God will help me to see people as indivduals, not just as one of a group.

__ I will pray that God will reveal to me any areas of prejudicial thinking of which I am unaware.

Chapter 6

Thinking What

Is Pure

I remember an advertisement for Ivory Soap years ago that promised it was "99 44/100 percent pure." I never was sure what was pure about that soap, but I was always impressed that anything could be so almost totally pure. The advertisement gave you the feeling that if you used Ivory Soap, your skin would be pure and beautiful because the soap was so pure.

That was a good marketing slogan that sold a lot of soap because every woman wanted to have pure skin, whatever that was. I used a lot of Ivory Soap, but I was disappointed to discover that its claim of purity didn't seem to do any great wonders for me and my skin. I never looked like the Ivory Soap girl, with her translucent complexion and flawless skin.

Don't you wish we could buy a bar of soap that would make us pure inside? I would settle for 99 44/100 percent any day, but there is no such quick fix for purity in our lives. Purity begins with cleaning up our thoughts so that they are without contamination, clean, spotless, unblemished.

Proverbs 15:26 tells us: "The Lord detests the thoughts of the wicked, but those of the pure are pleasing to him." God knows our thoughts, both good and evil, and we have the privilege of pleasing Him with purity of thoughts. So let's take a closer look at exactly what it means to think about what is pure.

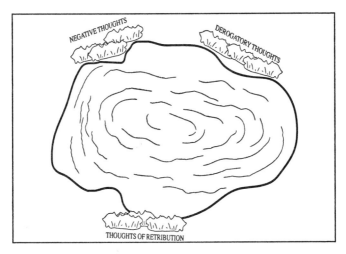

Impure Doctrine

Doctrine may sound like a theological word reserved for serious Bible students, but it is a word all of us should understand and embrace. Our doctrine is the body of beliefs we hold as truth. Of course, anyone can believe any doctrine he or she chooses. But for a Christian, our doctrine must be clearly based on what the Bible teaches. Otherwise, we are simply believing our own opinions and calling them doctrine.

Not long ago I was invited to speak to a large group of women. The invitation was worded in such a way that I knew they wanted me to guard carefully what I said so as not to offend anyone. They didn't want me to sound too "biblical" or use terminology that was unfamiliar or too "evangelistic."

While I agree that we Christians can often talk a "Christianese" vocabulary that is full of clichés and irrelevant to many, I know that if I don't present the pure truth of Scripture so that it is unmistakable, I will have failed my calling and my purpose. And furthermore, I will have failed my audience because no matter how entertaining my message may be, if it does not clearly set forth biblical truth, I've wasted people's time and done nothing more than tickle their ears. I've given them nothing of substance; nothing that can make a difference in their lives.

As a teacher, therefore, I have a heavy responsibility to teach pure doctrine—beliefs—untainted by opinion or trends or pop psychology or anything else that would contaminate the purity of God's Word. That means, of course, that I must know in depth what the Bible teaches. That's the only way I can be certain that I'm presenting pure doctrine.

Jesus avoided impure doctrine.

It is extremely important for every Christian to have a clear and pure understanding of biblical principles and a strong commitment never to compromise that doctrine. Jesus never watered down truth. In fact, in John 6:48-69 we read of a specific occasion when Jesus made a doctrinally pure statement and lost many followers as a result.

After He had described the true meaning of discipleship—that He was the living bread and that "unless you eat the flesh of the Son of Man and drink his blood, you have no life in you" (John 6:53)—many disciples complained that it was a "hard teaching." They didn't like this doctrinally pure statement; it was uncomfortable; it upset the status quo; it demanded commitment and dedication that they were not prepared to give.

> Aware that his disciples were grumbling about this, Jesus said to them, "Does this offend you? What if you see the Son of Man ascend to where he was before! The Spirit gives life; the flesh counts for nothing. The words I have spoken to you are spirit and they are life. Yet there are some of you who do not believe."
>
> John 6:61-64

Even though the truth offended them, Jesus gave it to them because contained in it were words of life. Pure doctrine was exactly what they needed to find life, yet:

> From this time many of his disciples turned back and no longer followed him.
>
> John 6:66

His insistence on purity of doctrine caused Jesus to lose disciples, but He never altered His teaching based on popularity contests or the latest opinion polls. Only truth would set people free, so He gave pure truth. Jesus is the only religious leader I know of who consistently thinned His ranks. He never got involved in the numbers game. He wasn't deluded into equating popularity with success.

On seeing the exodus of followers, Jesus asked the Twelve if they were going to leave Him, too. This is one time Simon Peter had the right answer: "Lord, to whom shall we go? You have the words of eternal life. We believe and know that you are the Holy One of God" (John 6:68-69).

Purity of doctrine gives us words of life, not Band-Aids to put on cancers. Truth sets us free, as Jesus told us in John 8:32. When our beliefs are pure, they are free from false doctrine and man-made opinions or ideas. We are, therefore, believing the truth and that will set us free from the consequences of believing something that is not true, as we discussed in chapter 3. Since truth sets us free, error binds us and holds us prisoners. Purity of doctrine is essential to our freedom in Christ.

Paul wrote to young Timothy:

> As I urged you when I went into Macedonia, stay there in Ephesus so that you may command certain men not to teach false doctrines any longer nor to devote themselves to myths and endless genealogies. These promote controversies rather than God's work—which is by faith. The goal of this command is love, which comes from a pure heart and a good conscience and a sincere faith.
>
> 1 Timothy 1:3-5

We can avoid impure doctrine.

Polluted doctrine promotes controversies and creates dissension within the body of Christ and within a person. Interestingly, when our minds are polluted with false doctrine, we do not know it because we are deceived. Being deceived is a condition of which we are always unaware; if we knew we were deceived, we would no longer be deceived. We need, therefore, to be very cautious about what we believe and continually search God's Word for any areas where we may be deceived. It is a good daily exercise to ask God for the wisdom and discernment to recognize any areas of deceit in our lives, especially as related to our beliefs.

We Christians can be easily deceived when we do not have a firm grip on the truth of God's Word. There is no substitute for Bible knowledge. Doctrine and theology are not just for preachers or teachers or highly educated people. A thorough understanding of biblical doctrine is essential if we want to have purity of beliefs and not be led astray by false doctrine.

Typically we think of false doctrine as weird cultist beliefs for which we would never fall. But we have an Enemy who is much slicker than that. He disguises false doctrine in very palatable ways so that the average Christian will buy into it. It may look good and sound good.

A friend told me of a group of people who have started a church in the Chicago area and their doctrine is solid and true to God's Word in some major areas. But they have combined that true doctrine with some very false doctrine, which they emphasize strongly. Coupled with a very empathetic and caring approach, this group has been quite successful at luring people away from Bible-believing congregations. These people have been led into false doctrine because they don't know the truth of what the Bible really says.

The average Christian is also in great danger of being led astray by good-sounding psychological theories and beliefs, which dilute the truth of Scripture or adapt it to fit these theories. For example, the whole teaching about pursuing good self-esteem has been a major stumbling block to many people. This term *self-esteem* probably has a hundred different meanings to different people, but I believe it has many times been a successful tool of the Enemy to lead some people into a self-focused, self-seeking path that always leads to misery and failure. If you search the Scriptures, you'll discover that "self" is our problem, not our answer. And you'll find that we are to die to this "self" and put others ahead of "self," and think of others as more important than "self."

How often we hear people analyze their problems as "low self-esteem." Perhaps it comes from our society's victim mentality—we look for ways to avoid blame and shift the responsibility for our failures or shortcomings to something or someone else. "Low self-esteem" seems to be an easy scapegoat. Frankly, what is labeled as low self-esteem is more often what the Bible calls sin. When we are not living in obedience to the principles of Scripture and are not loyal to Jesus Christ, we're going to suffer "low self-esteem."

Purity of doctrine will help you avoid the pitfalls and dangers of being swept away by the pop philosophies that our society buys into and advances as truth. Remember that if we want to be pure in heart—pure in mind—we must be willing to accept pure doctrine, even if it requires changes in some long-held, cherished beliefs.

Sexual Impurity

In our society we are exposed to sexual exploitation at every turn. The minds of Americans—and most people in other countries—are continually bombarded with the notion of sex. Is it any wonder that we see so many sex crimes, widespread sexual infidelity, and great numbers of sexually transmitted diseases? We would have to live the life of a hermit to avoid being exposed to this sexual display.

What is frightening to me is that many American Christians—or at least those who call themselves Christians—seem to hold to sexual principles that are not much different from those of the world around us. I recently received a letter from a single woman who wants desperately to be married to a certain man in her church. For privacy reasons I can't relate all the details, but I was alarmed to see this woman's attitude toward illicit sex. She seemed to have no awareness of God's principles of purity. In fact, she talked about her relationship with God and her illicit relationship with this man in the same sentence, as though the two were compatible. My reply to her probably shocked her, but she had asked for a response, and in faithfulness to God's Word, I had to directly confront this wrong thinking on her part.

What do you think has caused this woman—and many others who are part of our Christian community—to have such a warped and unbiblical view of sexual purity? Sadly, these people have swallowed the world's message and failed to pursue a knowledge of God and His principles so their thinking has become totally polluted on this subject. Once we allow our thinking to become so impure, the message of purity will sound very strange to our ears.

Many times I've received letters from single Christian women asking for my advice about their boyfriends who are pushing them to have premarital sex. In most cases these boyfriends claim to be Christians, but they still insist that it will be okay to have premarital sex because both people really love each other and intend to be married. Though I've received many of these letters, I'm still shocked when I read them. Frankly, no true Christian woman should even have to ask for advice in this kind of situation. There's no need to pray for wisdom about what you should do. The Bible is so clear on this that the only thing we have to do is obey. Consider these three verses, for example:

> But a man who commits adultery lacks judgment; whoever does so destroys himself. Blows and disgrace are his lot, and his shame will never be wiped away.
>
> Prov. 6:32-33

> Let us behave decently, as in the daytime, not in orgies and drunkenness, not in sexual immorality and debauchery, not in dissension and jealousy.
>
> Rom. 13:13

You shall not commit adultery.

Ex. 20:14

My response to each of these letters has been a strong urging that these women immediately break off these relationships and have nothing further to do with these men. Any person who would urge you to do what you know is unscriptural is someone you need to avoid like the plague! Yet I know this advice sounds terribly old-fashioned and drastic to most people. And I fear that far too many Christian women go the way of the world and suffer terrible consequences for their impure lifestyles.

Sexual impurity starts in our minds.

Have you started to think about sexual purity by the world's standards? That is the place that impure sexual behavior begins. Oh, how we need to bring our thoughts back onto the frozen surface and think with purity when it comes to sexual matters.

Notice that I did not say that we should avoid thinking about sex. Sex, as intended by God for those who are married, is a beautiful expression of love and oneness, and those who are married can think about sex with their married partner without overstepping the boundary of "pure."

In what we call His Sermon on the Mount, Jesus addressed this issue of purity of thought when it comes to sex: "You have heard that it was said, 'Do not commit adultery.' But I tell you that anyone who looks at a woman lustfully has already committed adultery with her in his heart" (Matt. 5:27-28).

There's that term *heart* again, used to indicate a person's mind and thoughts. You and I can commit adultery or fornication in our minds. I doubt if this warning was intended solely for men; women certainly have the same opportunities for mental adultery or mental fornication.

If you're wondering what kind of sexual thoughts are out of bounds, anything you're thinking of that would be wrong to do is impure sexual thinking. As long as your thoughts do not exceed God's principles of acceptable sexual practice, then they remain sexually pure.

Another question I'm often asked is about masturbation. I am not an educated authority in these matters, but it seems to me that masturbation would almost always involve impure thinking. That would be a strong indication that it is not God's way to deal with our sexual drives.

It is a lie from Satan that a person cannot live without sexual activity—and I'm referring to normal, regular people who have the same needs and desires as you and I do. Our world has come to believe that you can't get along without "it." That is a lie that will lead you to terrible bondage. As we are told in 1 Corinthians 6, sexual sins have a particularly detrimental effect in our lives. They are no more sinful than other sins, but they are sins against our bodies, and as believers our bodies are the temple of God's Holy Spirit. That makes sexual sin particularly damaging and harmful. Paul says, "Flee from sexual immorality" (1 Cor. 6:18). Run from it and run fast.

If we allow sexually illicit thinking to hang around our minds very long, we will soon indulge in that sin. And once we start down the road of impure sexual behavior, it will hold an addiction and power over us that is stronger than almost any other addiction I can name. That's why we should flee it as though it were a vicious animal out to destroy us. It does destroy.

No doubt you know of someone right now who has ruined his or her life and probably damaged many others because of an affair of some description. That destruction began in that person's thought life. He or she would never have become involved in that sinful behavior if he or she had not first allowed impure thoughts to invade his or her mind. In the thought process, that affair began to look very attractive and very harmless. In the thinking stage, it seemed reasonable, irresistible, beautiful, fulfilling. But the consequences have brought chaos, shame, and great pain to many people. It all began with wrong thinking.

We can think purely about sex.

How do we keep our thoughts sexually pure? John gives us some good advice:

> Dear friends, now we are children of God, and what we will be has not yet been made known. But we know that when he appears, we shall be like him, for we shall see him as he is. Everyone who has this hope in him purifies himself, just as he is pure.
>
> 1 John 3:2-3

The hope that purifies our thoughts is our sure knowledge that we will see Jesus and be like Him. It is the hope we have of heaven. With this hope in us, our thoughts will be pure. If we're thinking about seeing Jesus and being like Him, if we're focusing our minds on the reality that Jesus might come today to take us with Him, if we are "heavenly minded," our thoughts will be pure. We cannot think sexually impure thoughts while at the same time thinking about seeing Jesus.

The psalmist also knew the way to sexual purity: "How can a young man keep his way pure? By living according to your word" (Ps. 119:9). We bring purity into our lives by living according to God's Word. That means we have to know it and then we must obey what we know. When we know what God wants us to do as clearly defined in the Bible, and when we willingly obey, our lives naturally become pure.

Notice the reference in this verse to a "young man." I think the emphasis here is on "young" not "man." By that I mean that it is in our younger years when sexual temptation has its strongest pull. If you're still in those young years, whether male or female, you need to recognize that you are in the most vulnerable time of your life when it comes to your sex drive.

I remember an older person telling me that sex has been "greatly overrated." I could agree with that statement at this stage of my life, but I recognize that when you're in the throes of those years of strong sex drive, hearing that sex is "greatly overrated" won't help you a bit!

You can take some steps to help yourself. Never touch pornography of any description—avoid it like the plague that it is. Stay clear of movies or television programs that treat sex casually or explicitly. Do not participate in sexual jokes, conversations, or innuendoes, and avoid people who do. And keep a very close watch on your thought life. Stay away from sexual fantasies; don't imagine what sex would be like with some person to whom you are attracted; don't start mentally undressing someone who has an attractive body. You get the idea! It's all in your mind, and you can commit adultery or fornication in your mind! Above all else, strive to live every moment of every day according to the Word of God.

Can you imagine the problems, heartaches, broken homes and relationships, pain, and suffering that could have been totally avoided if the people involved had learned the principle of thinking only what is pure? Purity of thought and mind leads to a life free from guilt and destruction. The cesspool that awaits you when you skate off the pond into impure thoughts is stinking and rotten. It has a thin coating that looks inviting, but you will quickly find yourself engulfed in slime and filth that is like a quicksand of the mind, pulling you under before you realize what has hit you.

Think About It

Do you have some cherished opinions or long-held philosophies that may be impure—meaning, they may not be totally in line with God's truth? If so, note those below:

My guess is you probably haven't listed anything above. Very few of us would be foolish enough to hold onto a belief we know is wrong. Remember, the problem with deception is that we don't know we are being deceived. So, the only way we can discover deception in our minds is to be open to God's Spirit, asking Him to reveal these deceptions to us.

Are you willing to ask God to reveal any areas in your beliefs or opinions where you are in any way deceived? If so, pray the following prayer, or one like it, every day for at least a week:

Dear Lord:

I know that purity of heart and mind must be founded on purity of doctrine. And I know that You are the only One who can show me what is truly in my heart and mind. Please show me how I have been deceiving myself. I want to be free from the impurity of belief that those deceptions are causing.

Amen.

Now, what steps can you take to shore up your knowledge of biblical truth?

__ I can increase the time I spend in the Word by fifteen minutes each day.

__ I can take a correspondence Bible study course.

__ I can take an evening class in a Bible school.

__ I can become part of a local Bible study group.

__ I can buy and read some trusted books on biblical doctrine.*

Answer the following questions with a yes or a no:

__ Do I believe some sexual activity is acceptable outside the boundaries of marriage?

__ Do I tolerate books, movies, conversations, jokes, television programs, etc., that depict and/or legitimize sexually impure lifestyles?

__ Do I allow myself to look at sexually explicit magazines, etc.?

__ Have I committed adultery or fornication in my mind with women or men to whom I am attracted?

If you answered yes to any of the questions above, what steps do you need to take so that your thoughts will become sexually pure? Check any statements that apply.

__ I need to change my television/movie viewing habits.

__ I need to burn some books and/or magazines.

__ I need to avoid certain people whose conversations are in the gutter.

__ I need some one-on-one Christian counsel to help me find freedom from my sexual addictions.

When will you take this action?

*Some suggestions:
Mere Christianity by C. S. Lewis
Knowing God by J. I. Packer
Know Why You Believe by Paul E. Little
More Than a Carpernter by Josh McDowell

Chapter 7

THINKING WHAT IS

LOVELY AND ADMIRABLE

Quite some time ago a friend of mine was traveling on a bus in New York City with her sister. They were born in Sweden, and their family moved to the United States when they were teenagers. As they were riding together on the bus, they began to converse in their mother tongue, Swedish. My friend Tina noticed a woman on the bus who was wearing a very funny hat. They assumed no one else on the bus could understand Swedish, so they felt free to make fun of the woman's hat. She and her sister made several rather snide and uncomplimentary remarks about the hat, laughing quite freely, enjoying the joke at the woman's expense.

As the woman with the funny hat stood up to get off the bus, she turned to Tina and her sister and in perfect Swedish told them what she thought about their comments! You can imagine how shocked and embarrassed they both were. They never intended for the woman to understand their comments; they certainly never dreamed she understood Swedish.

This story could just as easily have been told about two people and their thoughts. How often we rationalize to ourselves that as long as no one knows what we're thinking, we can think whatever we like. After all, we're thinking in a language others cannot understand, we reason. So, if we see someone who is dressed in poor taste, we can think about how terrible that person looks, and no harm has been done because we didn't say what we were thinking, right? If we're listening to a speaker or preacher, we can silently criticize the sermon or speech, think about how we could do it better, etc., etc. After all, no one will know because we can think those kind of thoughts while keeping a smile on our faces and looking pleasant.

Motivation to Eliminate Unlovely Thoughts

One of the concepts that has motivated me to dig deep into the recesses of my mind and start examining and cleaning out my thoughts is the reality that every thought I ever have is totally and fully known by God. Before it is on my mind, He knows what I'm thinking! As the psalmist reminds us:

> The Lord knows the thoughts of man; he knows that they are futile.
>
> Ps. 94:11

> O Lord, you have searched me and you know me. You know when I sit and when I rise; you perceive my thoughts from afar. You discern my going out and my lying down; you are familiar with all my ways. Before

a word is on my tongue you know it completely, O Lord.

Ps. 139:1-4

Here is a prayer from an old, out-of-print book which I have written in my prayer journal:

"Lord, rid me of all thoughts that I would not write on my forehead with indelible ink. Thus my thoughts are written on my soul, for thee to see—for all to see, some day" (Amos Wells, *When Thou Has Shut Thy Door*. Fleming H. Revell Company, p. 38).

In Matthew 9:1-8 we read one of several incidents in the Bible where we are told that Jesus knew the thoughts of people. In this case some of the teachers of the law thought to themselves, *"This fellow is blaspheming!"* because Jesus had told a paralytic that his sins were forgiven. Verse 4 says: "Knowing their thoughts, Jesus said, 'Why do you entertain evil thoughts in your hearts?'"

Can you imagine how shocked those teachers must have been when Jesus revealed their thoughts? They didn't realize that Jesus could read their minds, and they certainly never intended for Him to tell everyone else in earshot what they were thinking!

To tell the truth, I wouldn't have wanted to be in their shoes, having Jesus broadcast my thoughts for all to hear. Most of us would feel embarrassed to think that others might know some of our private thoughts. Like my friend Tina, who indulged in unlovely words, we indulge in unlovely thoughts because we never intend for others to know. Yet, why hasn't it dawned on us that God already knows every thought we have? Why aren't we embarrassed and shamed to realize that Jesus knows all the unkind, unlovely thoughts we entertain?

Paul asked the Galatians, "Am I now trying to win the

approval of men, or of God? Or am I trying to please men?" (Gal. 1:10). And he answered those questions in his first letter to the Thessalonians: "We are not trying to please men but God, who tests our hearts" (1 Thes. 2:4). I encourage you, as I do myself, to ask those same questions of yourself. Is it more important to you to be accepted and approved by people, or to please the Lord? If you would not want all of your thoughts broadcast to the people around you, how much more should you be concerned that every one of them is broadcast to the Lord?

Of course, the truth is that when I try to please Jesus, I end up pleasing more people in the process than I would if I deliberately tried to please people. So, we really don't have to choose between pleasing people or God. Proverbs 16:7 says, "When a man's ways are pleasing to the Lord, he makes even his enemies live at peace with him." But when we are more concerned about pleasing people than we are about pleasing God, we usually miss on both fronts.

If the idea of having all of your thoughts written with indelible ink on your forehead for all to see is distasteful or uncomfortable to you (and it is to me), ask God to give you a greater sensitivity to the fact that all of your thoughts are written for Him to see. I have found that by focusing on that knowledge—God knows what I'm thinking right now—I am developing a growing desire to please God in my thought life. I have a new desire to clean out my unlovely thoughts so that I can please Him.

Also, think about this. Even though your thoughts are not written on your forehead with indelible ink for all to see, they are written in your words, your actions and reactions, your body language, your facial expressions, etc. Whatever you are thinking will almost always be communicated to those around you in some way or another, consciously or unconsciously.

Lovely and admirable thoughts are those that could be written on your forehead and that you wouldn't be ashamed or embarrassed for all to see.

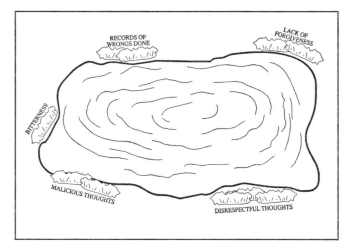

Whatever Is Lovely

Many times our thoughts may pass all the other tests of the Philippians 4:8 passage, but they'll fall short on this point. Let's try to get a handle on exactly what lovely thinking is.

Lovely is defined in my dictionary as "having a beauty that appeals to the heart as well as to the eye" *(Random House College Dictionary, 1980)*. With slight changes, we can use that same description to help us identify the nature of lovely thoughts. Lovely thoughts appeal to the heart as well as to the mind. Lovely thoughts are full of love. Not mushy, Hollywood love, but agape love. Lovely thoughts produce actions of love.

Actions of love are beautifully described in the famous love chapter of the Bible, 1 Corinthians 13:

Love is patient, love is kind. It does not envy, it does not boast, it is not proud. It is not rude, it is not self-seeking, it is not easily angered, it keeps no record of wrongs. Love does not delight in evil but rejoices with the truth. It always protects, always trusts, always hopes, always perseveres.

1 Cor. 13:4-7

Before we can demonstrate agape love, we must learn to think with agape love. Let's look at two of these qualities of lovely thinking.

Lovely thinking keeps no record of wrongs.

Isn't it amazing how we can forget so much we should remember, but it takes no effort at all to remember the wrongs done to us, the unkind word, the pain of our past, our hurt feelings. That memory bank of ours seems to have endless capacity to store away these records of wrongs.

Can you think of any records of wrongs done to you that are currently stored away in your mind? Some of the things on that mental record you've been keeping may have been very harmful and hurtful. You may feel justified in your feelings toward the one who has wronged you. But if you allow those thoughts of wrong done to you to continue to occupy your mind, they will turn on you and cause you additional pain and suffering.

To think lovely thoughts, we must learn to forgive those who have wronged us. And we must forgive, even if the one who has wronged us never asks us for forgiveness. I know that seems almost impossible and indeed it is to our natural selves, but God can give us the power to forgive others the way He forgives us.

Forgiveness begins in our minds. We can verbalize forgiveness, but we'll never reap the benefits of forgiveness until we stop keeping those mental records of the wrongs done to us. That doesn't mean that we erase our memories. Only God has the ability to forgive and forget. It does, however, mean that we release the record keeping to God and choose to stop thinking about the harm done to us.

When we keep records of wrongs done to us we magnify them. Our minds have this strange ability to amplify and embellish the pain. The more we think about something, the worse it seems. I've known people who focused so much on past pain they eventually found their identity in their suffering. They see themselves as victims and every aspect of their living is tainted by this pain-ridden past. Perhaps without realizing it, they have hung onto the harms of their past as a way of gaining pity and attention and as a way of avoiding responsibilities and duties.

My very good friend, now a widow, confirms that forgiveness is the way to healing. She was married for almost forty years to a man who was not a believer, and there were many difficult days in her marriage. Yet she kept trusting in the Lord and raising her children to know the Lord. Time and again it was necessary to forgive her husband for things he said and did that were hurtful. But she says that God was faithful to help her forget those things. Even before his death, her memory of the wrongs done to her faded. She could remember that there were some hard times, but she no longer could recall the details or specifics. She is convinced that God has given her the gift of forgetting the wrongs done to her, and therefore set her free from the pain of those wrongs.

In John 5:1-15 we find the well-known story of the healing of an invalid man at the pool of Bethesda. According to local belief at that time, the first person into this pool when the waters were mysteriously and unpredictably stirred would be healed of his or her disease or disability. For thirty-eight years this invalid had been by the pool, but he was not healed, supposedly because he never got into the pool first.

Jesus asked him, "Do you want to get well?" (John 5:6) Have you ever wondered why Jesus asked a crippled man such a question? Wasn't it obvious that he wanted to be well? Why else would he sit beside this pool for thirty-eight years?

Well, look at it another way. How could he possibly not manage to get in that pool first in thirty-eight long years? If he really wanted to be well, in thirty-eight years he surely could have figured some method to get into that pool before anyone else did, even if he had to sit in the pool all the time or hire several people to sit with him and put him in the pool when it stirred.

Now, whether or not this would have healed him, we aren't told. I think it was some old wives' tale or custom, and I rather doubt that just getting into that water guaranteed healing. Regardless, if this invalid truly believed the water would heal him and if he really wanted to be healed, don't you think he would have somehow managed to get in that pool first in a span of thirty-eight years?

Jesus understood that not everyone truly wants to be healed. Some people don't want the responsibility that comes with healing. After all, if this man were well, he'd have to find a job and take care of himself. He'd have no more excuses. No longer could he shift the blame as he did in verse 7:

"'Sir, the invalid replied, 'I have no one to help me into the pool when the water is stirred. While I am trying to get in, someone else goes down ahead of me.'"

In other words, it wasn't his fault that he was still crippled. No one in thirty-eight years was willing to help him into the pool! That's a story that is a little difficult to believe if you ask me! Later, when Jesus saw him at the temple, He told him, "See, you are well again. Stop sinning or something worse may happen to you" (John 5:14). We aren't told what sin he was committing, but Jesus made it clear that this man's sin had contributed to his handicap.

In a similar way, when we willfully keep records of wrongs done to us, we are refusing to get well and contributing to our own pain. It is self-inflicted suffering. And keeping records of wrongs done to us always results in bitterness.

The writer to the Hebrews warns us about bitterness: "See to it that no one misses the grace of God and that no bitter root grows up to cause trouble and defile many" (Heb. 12:15). Where do bitter roots grow? In the garden of our minds. When we let bitter roots grow, we miss the grace of God. We no longer enjoy the benefits of God's grace in our lives—benefits such as contentment, peace, and joy. And when bitter roots are allowed to grow in our minds, they will cause us much trouble and defile many others as well.

I know that many of you have good reason to be bitter toward people who have wronged you. Perhaps these people have never even asked you to forgive them. They may even be continuing to treat you wrongly. And I recognize that forgiving those wrongs done to you may be extremely difficult. In fact, it may look like mission impossible to you.

Forgiveness is perhaps the most difficult thing God asks us to do. It is difficult primarily because it seems as if we're letting people off the hook when they don't deserve to be let off the hook! Maybe you're thinking, *After all the harm these people have done to me, how can I just forgive them and that's the end of it?* Be sure, however, to remember this: These people may be off your hook, but they are not off God's hook. Paul told us: "Do not take revenge, my friends, but leave room for God's wrath, for it is written: 'It is mine to avenge; I will repay,' says the Lord" (Rom. 12:19).

When you refuse to forgive, you cannot think rightly because your mind is full of the wrongs done to you. From that comes bitterness, which always backfires on you, and then you usually start trying to repay those who have harmed you. When you and I try to avenge, we get in God's way and we don't "leave room for God's wrath." Trust me, God is much better at repaying people for the wrong they have done than you are. Leave room for Him to work.

As difficult as forgiveness is, there is one thing more difficult and that is refusing to forgive. Your thought life will never be lovely until you give God permission to help you stop keeping records of the wrongs done to you. Are you willing to end that suffering? It's your choice.

One good way to change those bitter, unlovely thoughts is to think about Jesus. Think of how He was treated so wrongly. Remember the abuse and disgrace that He suffered unfairly. Peter tells us how Jesus responded to those who mistreated Him:

> To this you were called, because Christ suffered for you, leaving you an example, that you should follow in his steps. "He committed no sin, and no deceit was found in his mouth." When they hurled their insults at him, he did not retaliate; when he suffered, he made no threats. Instead, he entrusted himself to him who judges justly.
>
> 1 Peter 2:21-23

He entrusted himself to His Father, the One Who always makes right and just judgments. Jesus, therefore, didn't have to retaliate; He didn't have to prove His point; He didn't have to have the last word because He knew that the Father was still in control and that He would avenge in the right time and the right way. He "entrusted." That's the key word.

Can you entrust your past to the One Who can handle it? When you are able to do that, your self-inflicted suffering caused by keeping those records of the wrongs done to you will start to end. Because those records are in your mind, the healing must begin in your thought life. You must choose to stop thinking the unlovely thoughts that are focused on the wrong done to you. If Jesus could do this, and He suffered more than any of us ever will, you can do the same by the power of God within you.

Lovely thinking desires the good of others.

First Corinthians 13:6-7 says, "Love does not delight in evil but rejoices with the truth. It always protects, always trusts, always hopes, always perseveres." Lovely thinking means wanting good things to happen to other people. It means not delighting when others are in trouble, even if they deserve the trouble they are in. Lovely thinking means protecting others from harm, if possible, and always hoping for the best to happen to others.

Can you think of any recent occasions when you've found yourself hoping that someone would get "what he or she deserves"? Some have demonstrated that attitude toward people with AIDS, even some Christians. That, of course, is not lovely thinking. Where would you be if you got what you deserved? Where would I be?

In my mind I can imagine how people who have hurt me are going to get their comeuppance. I can play out scenarios of how bad things are going to happen to them, how I'm going to have an opportunity to tell them off, how they are going to find out that they've been found out! After all, they deserve to be punished, and if I cannot punish them in real life, I can at least do so in my thoughts. And when I do, I get a momentary feeling of justice, of being vindicated, of getting what is due me, and I like those feelings.

That kind of thinking is not lovely thinking, and it will eventually start to work on my mind, eating away at me, raising my stress levels, making me bitter and angry, changing my appearance, damaging relationships—the list goes on.

How can we ever reach the point in our thought lives where we actually want others to be blessed, to be prosperous, to be delivered from trouble, even though they have created some problems in our lives? It is a mission impossible without the power of God's Holy Spirit. But when you can get to this stage in cleaning up your thought life, you have made great progress, and you will see God's blessings on you in new and amazing ways.

First, identify those people whom you would like to see get what they deserve. Write their names down. Then by faith, not by feelings, begin praying for them regularly. Pray that God will bless them. When you do that, you are directly obeying our Lord's command: "Bless those who curse you, pray for those who mistreat you" (Luke 6:28).

Think of specific blessings for those people and pray that good things will happen to them. "Lord, I pray that she will have favor with the boss and get that promotion she wants so badly." "Lord, I pray he'll do well on his exam and get a good grade." "Lord, please send her the money she needs at this time." Pray very specific prayers of blessings on their lives. You will discover that this changes your thoughts about these people.

Don't be surprised to discover that this process takes time. There is likely to be a battle in your mind when you determine to put away the unlovely thoughts. Don't be discouraged when you frequently have to go back and do this all over again because those unlovely thoughts have crept back into your mind. When we start changing our thought patterns, we are breaking old, well-established habits of thinking, and they don't break easily. But every time you pray for those who mistreat you and force yourself to ask God to bless them, you are building spiritual muscle in your mind that will enable you to start really thinking in loving and lovely ways, genuinely wanting goodwill to come to even those who make your life difficult.

When that begins to happen, you will know that the power of God is working in your life because you could never do that in your own power. And then you will become excited about the transformation you are seeing in yourself. It will amaze you and give you great joy and peace to see that you can actually think lovely thoughts about people who are such a thorn in your flesh.

Lovely thinking is transforming and benefits us as much as it does those to whom our loving thoughts are directed. Obviously, this kind of thinking will dramatically change the way we treat other people, the tone of voice in which we speak to them, the body language we display when they are around. And that will usually result in improved relationships.

You see, when we start this process of examining our thoughts to see if they match the guideline of lovely, we begin to understand that this kind of thinking is not just to make us treat others better and be better Christians. It is also our avenue to freedom. It releases us from those harmful and painful thought patterns that have been a burden to us. It reduces our stress immensely. God's way is simply the best for everyone, and once we start to get a grip on that reality, lovely thinking becomes more and more attractive and possible.

Whatever Is Admirable

In addition to true, noble, right, pure, and lovely, our thoughts must be admirable. In Philippians 4:8 Paul adds two other words to define admirable—excellent and praiseworthy. I think he just wanted to be certain that we didn't miss the point here. Admirable thoughts are worthy of praise. To be admirable, our thoughts must be in good taste, refined, of a good reputation. This eliminates distasteful and disrespectful thinking.

Our American media are crammed with political satire and commentary, from television news programs to radio talk shows and newspaper columns, etc. And I must admit that I am a "news junkie."

As I began this process of examining my thought life, I began to realize how my mind had been polluted by the media with a great deal of disrespectful thinking toward people in political offices, from the President on down. I was convicted of how much my thoughts were full of criticism, cynicism, and condemnation toward those with whom I disagree.

Now, I believe my thoughts were true because, according to biblical principles, many of these politicians are making very wrong decisions and leading our country down destructive paths. Disrespectful thinking, however, doesn't solve anything, does it? And my mind was full of very disrespectful thoughts. They were not admirable.

How could my thoughts be admirable when the actions of the politicians were not admirable? How could I admire someone I don't admire? Consider what it means to have thoughts that are admirable. It doesn't mean you admire certain people; it means the way you think about them is admirable.

Admirable thoughts toward people who are not admirable are thoughts of compassion and concern. What I've tried to begin to do is pray for these politicians that they will become convicted and see the error of their ways. That is an admirable thought. I wouldn't be ashamed to tell anyone that I'm praying for these politicians. I wouldn't mind if those thought prayers were displayed in indelible ink on my forehead because they are admirable thoughts. And of course, praying for these politicians will reap benefits, where disrespectful thinking only causes me more frustration and stress and gets me entangled in the bushes off the frozen surface.

Who is it in your life that you do not respect? Your boss? Your mate? Your coworker? A family member? Think about how you think about that person or those people. Are your thoughts admirable? Likely not. They should be and can be whether the person is admirable or not.

Think About It

Who has wronged you? What records of wrongs done to you have you been keeping in your mind? Writing them down will force you to get out of denial and face the unlovely thoughts you've been storing in your mind. Are you willing to abandon your unlovely thought patterns of these people? When you are, enter the date of that decision in the last column as a reminder and a covenant with God that you have chosen, not by feelings but by faith, to forgive and clean out the unlovely thoughts that have been in your mind.

People Who Have Wronged Me	What They Did to Me	I Choose to Forgive Them

Are there some people whom you would like to see get what they deserve? In order to think lovely thoughts instead of malicious thoughts about these people, this exercise might be helpful.

Write down the names of these people. Then by faith, not by feelings, begin praying for them regularly. Pray that God will bless them. When you do that, you are directly obeying our Lord's command: "Bless those who curse you, pray for those who mistreat you" (Luke 6:28). Then think of specific blessings for those people and pray that good things will happen to them.

Name   Specific Blessing to Pray

_____   _____

_____   _____

_____   _____

_____   _____

_____   _____

_____   _____

_____   _____

_____   _____

Chapter 8

CONFORMING OUR THOUGHTS

TO PHILIPPIANS 4:8

A fter this intensive study of Philippians 4:8, I would not be surprised if you are feeling a bit overwhelmed at this point. I well remember when I first began to tackle this project of bringing my thoughts in line with God's Word. I felt as though I would be forever stuck in some of those bushes and bogs that lurked on the edges of my mental pond.

As you struggle with your thoughts, please remember two things. First, God never asks us to do more than we are able to do, by His grace. Philippians 4:8 would not be in the Bible if it were truly mission impossible. And second, remember that what God calls us to do, He then does in us and through us. Remember 1 Thessalonians 5:24: "The one who calls you is faithful and He will do it." Frankly, I wouldn't be motivated to clean up my thought life except that the Spirit of God living within me prompts me to do so. And I can only make changes in my thought life because of the power of that same Spirit.

Our part is to set our will to bring our thoughts into conformity with the truth of Philippians 4:8. God never forces us to do His will; He looks for willing obedience. But we must never lose sight of the reality that the only way true change will happen is for God to do it through us. We must delicately balance the set of our will, giving God permission and control, and then relying totally on His strength and power to work His will in us.

It seems that many people get to the "I really want to" stage, but they stumble at that point because they don't have any specific, concrete steps in mind that will put them on the road to transformed thinking. So, in this chapter I want to offer some additional suggestions and steps that will help you start to put the truth of Philippians 4:8 into practice in your life. Then you will be able to "skate" with freedom.

Keep in mind that this is a lifelong process, a lesson we will always be learning. None of us will ever "arrive" at totally cleaning up our thoughts, at least not until we get to heaven, where we will dump this old nature. We can, however, make wonderful progress on this earth if we will begin and take it one step at a time. Remember, the blessing is in the doing, not in the knowing, so if you will take step one, even if it's a baby step, then you'll start this very important and life-changing journey toward cleaning up your thought life and transforming your life. Don't forget, it's all in your mind!

Controlled by the Spirit

The Apostle Paul gave us some very insightful truth when he wrote this to the church at Corinth:

For who among men knows the thoughts of a man except the man's spirit within him? In the same way no one knows the thoughts of God except the Spirit of God. We have not received the spirit of the world but the Spirit who is from God, that we may understand what God has freely given us. This is what we speak, not in words taught us by human wisdom but in words taught by the Spirit, expressing spiritual truths in spiritual words. The man without the Spirit does not accept the things that come from the Spirit of God, for they are foolishness to him, and he cannot understand them, because they are spiritually discerned. The spiritual man makes judgments about all things, but he himself is not subject to any man's judgment: "For who has known the mind of the Lord that he may instruct him?" But we have the mind of Christ.

1 Cor. 2:11-16

As we ponder the seeming impossibility of thinking as Philippians 4:8 tells us to, we need to understand some key truths discussed in this passage in 1 Corinthians.

1. No other person can know exactly what you think because no other person has your spirit within him or her. In order to know someone's thoughts, we must have that person's spirit within us (vs. 11).

2. Those who have been born from above into God's family have received the Spirit Who is from God. We have His Spirit in us (vs. 12).

3. Because we have God's Spirit within us, we have the mind of Christ within us (vs. 16).

The mind-blowing truth is that we are given the Spirit of Christ—the same Spirit that raised Jesus from the dead—to dwell in our bodies as believers (Rom. 8:9-11). Have you ever really stopped to consider the impact of that one truth? You and I are incredibly privileged to have the Spirit of Christ within us, and because of that, we have a unique ability to know the mind of God.

As Paul pointed out, the only way we can know exactly what someone else thinks is to have that other person's spirit in us so that we can think his or her thoughts. There may be someone in your life that you know so well, you have said, "I know what you're thinking." And it may be true that your intimate knowledge of that person gives you the ability to frequently guess what she is thinking with accuracy. But that is knowledge that comes from experience with that person, not from an actual reading of her thoughts. You are taking very well-educated guesses. You could only truly read that person's mind if her spirit were inside of you so that your thoughts were the same as her thoughts.

But while we'll never be able to have the spirit of another person in us, we can and do have the Spirit of Christ within us. Result: we can know what Jesus is thinking, and we can think His thoughts! From my perspective, this is one of the most miraculous and marvelous gifts we have as believers.

If we have the Spirit of Christ in us and we can therefore think as Jesus does, why do we struggle with our thought lives? Shouldn't it then be easy for us to get rid of wrong thoughts and think only right ones, as Christ would?

Romans 7:14-25 explains this dilemma for us:

We know that the law is spiritual; but I am unspiritual, sold as a slave to sin. I do not understand what I do. For what I want to do I do not do, but what I hate I do. And if I do what I do not want to do, I agree that the law is good. As it is, it is no longer I myself who do it, but it is sin living in me. I know that nothing good lives in me, that is, in my sinful nature. For I have the desire to do what is good, but I cannot carry it out. For what I do is not the good I want to do; no, the evil I do not want to do—this I keep on doing. Now if I do what I do not want to do, it is no longer I who do it, but it is sin living in me that does it. So, I find this law at work: When I want to do good, evil is right there with me. For in my inner being I delight in God's law; but I see another law at work in the members of my body, waging war against the law of my mind and making me a prisoner of the law of sin at work within my members. What a wretched man I am! Who will rescue me from this body of death? Thanks be to God—through Jesus Christ our Lord! So then, I myself in my mind am a slave to God's law, but in the sinful nature a slave to the law of sin.

Paul describes a war here, the battle between our desire to do good and our propensity to do just the opposite. This battle continues even after we are born from above because while we indeed do acquire a new nature coming from the Spirit of Christ Who dwells within us, we still have the old sinful nature that we were born with (v. 18). And these two natures are at war within us; one wants to do good and the other wants to do evil.

Thankfully, in Romans 8:5 Paul gives us the good news of how we can win this battle between our two natures: "Those who live according to the sinful nature have their minds set on what that nature desires; but those who live in accordance with the Spirit have their minds set on what the Spirit desires."

Notice that the battle between these two natures takes place in our minds. It's all in our minds! When our minds are focused on what our old nature desires, then we think and behave as we used to, in a sinful and selfish way. When our minds are controlled by the Spirit of Christ Who dwells in us, then we think and behave as Jesus would because we are thinking and behaving in accordance with His Spirit within us.

Now, as in any battle, the stronger person will win. If you have a fight with someone twice your size, who is strong and well-trained while you are anemic and frightened, obviously the other person is highly likely to win that fight. When our old nature starts to battle with our new nature—and that battle is inevitable for all believers—the stronger nature will win.

So, in order to put into practice the truth of Philippians 4:8, we must make certain that our new nature, the one from God, is the strong one. We can do this by consciously starving the old nature so that it is weak and helpless while we feed the new one so that it is strong and healthy.

How do we feed these two natures? Which nature do you feed the most and best? Those are the questions we're going to consider now.

Guarding Against Mental Garbage

An important discipline we must learn to practice is to carefully guard what goes into our minds. This is step one on the road to transformed thinking.

You're probably aware of the expression "Garbage In, Garbage Out" (GIGO). It is a phrase that our computer age has generated, meaning that your computer can only give you good information and good results if the raw material that you program into your computer is accurate and complete.

Well, believe me, GIGO holds true for our minds as well. If you put garbage into your mind, your thought life will reflect that input. Are you programming your mind to think according to your sinful nature or according to the Spirit of God within you?

As a child you probably sang this song in church as I did:

Oh, be careful little eyes what you see,
Oh, be careful little eyes what you see,
For the Father up above is looking down in love,
So be careful little eyes what you see.

The second and third verses tell us to be careful little ears what you hear and be careful little feet where you go. Maybe we stopped singing this song too soon because the truth of this child's song is one we desperately need to practice as adults. What our eyes see, what our ears hear, and where our feet take us strongly influence our thinking; the input affects the output.

Be careful what you read.

Think about what you've read lately. It may be quite eye-opening for you to make a list of your reading material over the past thirty days and estimate the amount of time you've spent reading various types of material. You may learn some things about how you spend your reading time. I've included a chart for this purpose at the end of this chapter, so I encourage you to take time for this exercise.

In the last thirty days did you spend more time reading the Bible than everything else put together? I've tried to take that as my rule of thumb in deciding what I will read. Like many of you, I'm a book addict and can get lost for hours in a bookstore. In addition, many publishers send me review copies of their books, so my office and my home are stacked with good books that I want to read. But if I'm not careful, I'll spend more time with the "good books" than I do with the Good Book. It can become a trap, and we should always put our highest priority on consistently reading the Bible.

How much time do you spend reading good Christian material versus reading the world's literature, even if it's not necessarily evil? We need to be well-read and well-educated people, with interests in all of God's creation and the good things that we can pursue. But so much of what we read that is produced by the world is nothing but garbage, disguised by good writing skills, beautiful pictures, superb design, and attractive publications. Be very picky about what you read.

There are a few good novelists today who stay away from profanity and vulgarity. *A few*—and if you intend to read novels, you must choose very carefully. I picked up a novel not long ago by a famous American author and greatly looked forward to reading his book. He is a master storyteller, and his first book had been a delight that had filled up some boring airplane hours for me, so when I saw he had written a second book, I grabbed a copy with anticipation of more enjoyable reading.

I discovered, however, that he had changed his style greatly with his second book and ventured into a lot of sexual innuendo and narrative. After a few chapters, I was very uncomfortable with his book, and indeed it was nowhere near the quality of writing I had found in the first book. So, I threw it away (I didn't even want to sell it at a garage sale) and wrote a letter to this famous author telling him of my disappointment in his book.

Much to my surprise I received a response from him that was obviously personally typed. He said he appreciated my comments but defended the approach he took in his book. I was pleased he read my letter, and I am hopeful it caused him to realize that he didn't have to lower his standards. (By the way, his second book didn't sell nearly as well as his first. I think it might have been called a "flop.")

If you're reading something of the world's literature that

strays from the guidelines of "true, noble, right, pure, lovely, and admirable," I suggest that you close the covers, throw it away, and don't read anything by that author again. Just because you bought the book or checked it out of the library doesn't mean you have to read it. It's much better to throw away a few dollars than to fill your mind with profanity or sexual innuendo or whatever other garbage the book may contain.

There are many classic books that are very worthwhile reading, and few of us have read the classics as we should. Try *Little Women* or any of Jane Austen's books. Charles Dickens may be difficult to follow at times, but his books are worthwhile reading. I think we all need some "downtime" reading material occasionally, but if we are not careful, that downtime reading can pour lots of garbage into our minds, and that garbage is not easy to clean out.

A friend of mine told me of the damage done to her mind as she became addicted to the romance novels that are so prevalent today. They became an escape from the reality of her own life, and she got to the point where she was reading one or two a day! That's what I said—one or two a day. She had a night job that allowed her reading time, so all day and all night she was pouring this junk into her mind. And she became very addicted to those novels. (I have learned through her that many women are addicted to this worthless reading material and that these novels are produced in great proliferation and sold in the millions to these addicts.)

Finally, God's conviction in her heart caused her to get rid of every one of those books and to refuse to accept them from a neighbor who had passed them along to her for years. She told me how difficult it was to stop reading those trashy novels. She told of the damage it did to her marriage, of the struggle she began to have with immoral thoughts toward a man with whom she worked. It was not easy to quit, but God gave her the will and the power to do so, and today she never goes near that trash. I wish you could hear her testimony of the difference it has made in her life.

Oh, be careful little eyes what you read! It greatly influences what you think.

Be careful what you see.

Now, we start to go from "preachin' to meddlin'" here, as the old saying goes. What do you allow into your mind through movies and television? You realize, I'm sure, that what we take in through our eyes impacts us more strongly than any other kind of input. What we see really leaves a long-lasting impression; therefore, we truly need to be cautious in this area.

There is very little programming on television that is worthwhile. Yet, how often do you continue watching something that portrays illicit lifestyles, immorality, profanity, violence, sensuality? You are truly feeding and strengthening your old nature when you do this.

Think of what you have recently poured into your mind through movies and television. Again, you'll find another chart at the end of this chapter to help you document what you've been watching. I encourage you to take time to do that.

Now, here's the hard part. How much of what is on your watching list would pass our Philippians 4:8 test: true, noble, right, pure, lovely, and admirable? How often did you think, *I ought to shut this thing off or switch channels or walk out of this theater?* Did you do it?

If we spend very much time looking at television, chances are we're pouring lots of trash into our minds. Those soap operas and situation comedies are full of immorality and non-Christian lifestyles. That kind of steady diet as input into our minds will definitely have a negative impact on our thought life.

I know many Christians who are not picky about the movies they go to see. Even PG-rated movies are sometimes full of garbage, and you can be sure R-rated ones always are. Yet many Christians have no personal guidelines or prohibitions when it comes to the movies they watch.

As I am writing and editing this chapter, I am in a hotel in Southern California where I have been speaking at a women's conference. Like all hotel rooms, this one has movies available for rent, and there is one movie I was tempted to rent. It won several Academy Awards, and the television critics gave it rave reviews. But I saw that it is rated R and my long-standing rule has been that I don't even consider watching an R movie. But you know, I was strongly tempted because of the wide acceptance of this movie and the rave reviews it has received.

The irony of this did not escape my attention. As I am writing on the importance of carefully guarding what you watch, I am tempted to lower my standards and watch something inappropriate. It reminded me that this will always be a battle, and I can never let down my guard. I am thankful that I have set those standards and that I have told others I have those standards, which creates accountability. I'm also grateful God has given me the opportunity to write this book because it has strengthened my own commitment to go the extra mile in guarding what goes into my mind, and it means I have to be doubly sure that I practice what I preach.

Just because you're a Christian, you are not immune to the trash contained in those inappropriate movies. And believe me, the majority of movies produced by Hollywood are inappropriate for Christians. If you're going to the theater often or renting movies at the video store frequently, you've probably allowed much material into your mind that is not true, noble, right, pure, lovely, or admirable. You'll notice that when you do, your mind will be polluted for a very long time.

Be careful what you hear.

What music do you listen to? Are you soaking up the world's music? Much of those lyrics are absolutely sinful and sensual. Many people think that the lyrics don't really matter, and they claim to just like the beat of the music, but believe me, those lyrics get into your mind. If the lyrics don't meet the thought standards of true, noble, right, pure, lovely, and admirable, then you should never listen to that music.

What kind of conversations and casual talk do you listen to? For instance, what do you usually hear going on around you on your job or wherever you spend your daily hours? It's likely you are surrounded with these types of conversations:

Negative conversations
Critical conversations
Off-color jokes
Sexual innuendos
Gossip

My experience is that most work environments have more than their share of these kinds of conversations going on all the time. Now, if you're there in the midst of some of this, it's going into your head, right? And that's bound to affect the way you think.

What can you do when you find yourself exposed to such unlovely, unedifying conversations?

You can change the subject. Even if you sound abrupt, just redirect the conversation to something harmless.

You can walk away. If it's a group setting, you may be able to quietly walk away or get up and leave.

You can screen out the conversation. If you are in a spot where you cannot avoid overhearing an unedifying conversation, hum a tune to yourself or quote Scripture in your head to screen out the inappropriate conversation.

You can confront the people involved in the conversation. Say up front and out loud that you think the conversation is not edifying, and it makes you uncomfortable.

Most of us are far too easily intimidated by others in these kinds of situations, and we allow them to control conversations too easily. Jesus always associated with sinners, but I'm quite certain that His presence sent a message about what was appropriate and what was not appropriate to talk about. We should have such a reputation with our coworkers, family, and friends that they know where we draw the line when it comes to off-color jokes, gossip, slander, gripe sessions, sexual innuendos, etc.

I find that one of the more difficult areas for me is to know when I should take a bold stand. I am sensitive about hurting other people's feelings. I am aware that coming across as "Suzy Spiritual" will turn some people off. I don't want to give the impression that I'm some weird person from outer space or that I think I'm better than anyone else.

Yet, as a Christian living and working in a society which is very often anti-Christian, I have a strong responsibility to live by and uphold the principles of Scripture. Furthermore, I know that it is not good for me to allow garbage into my mind. If that garbage comes from the mouths of other people, then I've got to learn how to protect myself against it, while doing everything possible not to be offensive.

So, if I have to choose between being offensive and allowing garbage into my mind, I must take my stand against the garbage. I can't live a truly godly life in this world without offending some people. We have clear instructions in Scripture to be holy as God is holy (Lev. 11:44). If we truly pursue holiness, there's no way people around us can fail to notice the difference, and sometimes they may not like it. Our holy lives may cause them some uncomfortableness and convict them. They may take it out on us.

Once my lifestyle started to change dramatically some years ago after I recommitted my life to Christ and became serious about being His disciple, some people just dropped out of my life. They didn't like being around me. I truly tried not to offend them, but on the other hand, I could not deny the Lord who had redeemed me and was changing me so wonderfully. It caused some relationships to end, and it changed the nature of other relationships. Some people sensed they couldn't talk to me the way they used to, and that was uncomfortable for them.

Know the joy of a garbage-free mind.

Garbage in, garbage out. Please remember that you are responsible for what you allow into your mind, and whatever gets in becomes the fodder for your thought life. You can't allow sewage into your drinking water and not expect to get very sick. You can't allow garbage into your mind and not expect to have some very sick thoughts as a result.

If I have stepped on your toes a bit as we have explored what should and should not be allowed into our minds, believe me, I understand how you feel. When I started to examine the garbage going into my mind, I was extremely uncomfortable, and I didn't give in or give up easily. I didn't want to relinquish control of what I read, what I saw, what I talked about. I said to myself: *isn't this legalism, and haven't we been set free from the law?* I didn't want some strict rules that I had to live by! That old nature really resented the intrusion of Philippians 4:8 into my thought life and the limits it imposed on my thinking.

I wanted to rationalize it away. I wanted to tell myself that I could sift the good from the bad and not let the bad parts into my mind while enjoying only the good parts. I wanted to believe that I didn't have to apply this principle entirely in every circumstance because I knew it would really cause some drastic changes in my habits and lifestyle.

But I've come to understand that I cannot be lenient on myself in this area of "Garbage In" because I can't afford the clean-up process that's required once I let junk in. And I have to guard against "Garbage In" just as much now as when I first began. I don't expect I'll ever be able to let down my guard because my enemy, Satan, will continue to try to tempt me, and my old nature will still try to give in to those temptations.

But, as I starve that old nature, it has less success at controlling the input into my mind, and after a few years of practicing this, I've learned how much easier it is to keep the trash out in the first place. I'm actually finding that the garbage that used to tempt me holds less and less allurement as I experience the great joy of keeping my mind clean.

I encourage you not to go easy on yourself in this battle to control what goes into your mind. You may have some cancerous growths that can only be removed by major surgery, but if you don't remove them, if you only put a Band-Aid over them, they will come back to harm you and damage you spiritually. The Apostle Paul told us that if we "judged ourselves, we would not come under judgment" (1 Cor. 11:31). Here is the perfect opportunity for each of us to judge what garbage we are allowing into our minds and by God's grace, to start filtering it out.

Screening Our Thoughts

In order to "take captive every thought to make it obedient to Christ" (2 Cor. 10:5), we must deal with our thoughts on an individual basis, thought by thought. Notice that the Apostle

Paul says we are to take every thought and *make it* obedient to Christ. We are to force each individual thought to be obedient to Christ—the very principle discussed in Philippians 4:8.

When we *make* somebody do something, we are using force to overcome that person's reluctance. For example, as parents we have all had to make our children obey us, against their will and regardless of their objections. This is exactly the kind of struggle we are in with our thought life. Our individual thoughts are not going to voluntarily submit; we must learn how to take individual thoughts and make them obedient to Christ.

You can start this process by becoming very conscious of every thought you have. Ask God to make you sensitive to your thoughts. Don't be absent-minded—paying no attention to what you are thinking. Instead, be very thought-conscious. And then be prepared to make each thought obedient.

You are undoubtedly familiar with telephone screening in the business world. When bosses want certain unnecessary or annoying calls screened out, they subject callers to the screening process. This means that all callers first have to talk to a secretary who asks some questions to see if they meet the qualification of someone the boss will talk to.

I strongly urge you to do the same thing with your thoughts. As a thought approaches your mind and tries to make an entry into your head, make that thought go through the screening process. Think of it like a phone call.

Hello. What is your name, please? And what is the purpose of your call?

Are you an acceptable thought? Are you true, noble, right, pure, lovely, and admirable?

Oh, so sorry, you are true but you're not lovely and so this call cannot go through. Good-bye.

Hello. Are you a pure thought? No, I don't think so. You are calling to try to get me to do something that is not pure and right; therefore, I cannot talk to you. Good-bye.

I can almost hear some of you giggling or shaking your head as you read those screening examples. How silly, you may be thinking. Well, as I have stated already, I am simple-minded, and I'm always looking for ideas and techniques that will help me to put truth into practice. Otherwise, I know it but I don't do it, and the blessing comes in the doing! So, I pass this idea of screening your thoughts along to you as though they are phone calls because I know it can help you apply God's truth and see life-changing results.

Unless you have a better method of screening every individual thought and making it obedient to Christ, I encourage you to try this screening idea. I promise you, it will come in handy to help you remember to screen your thoughts one by one. We must start cleaning up our thoughts one by one on a daily basis.

Continuing this phone call analogy, you and I cannot control who calls us on the telephone. Likewise, you and I cannot totally control what thoughts try to enter our minds. We have an Enemy bombarding us with wrong thoughts, and we live in a culture full of wrong thinking. In addition, that old nature of ours produces wrong thinking. So we can expect wrong thoughts to dial our number and ring our bell. Answering the phone call is not the problem, but when we continue to talk to that wrong thought after we know its true nature, then we have crossed the line and allowed sin to enter the picture.

James 4:17 tells us: "Anyone, then, who knows the good he ought to do and doesn't do it, sins." Sin takes place when we recognize a wrong thought but fail to screen it out; when we are aware of its intrusion, and yet we do nothing to make it leave. That's when we fail, and then we've opened our minds to the garbage that will pollute our thinking.

Let me warn you that this point of decision is usually not easy. You'll find a real struggle going on within you, as you recognize your need to abandon the wrong thought. Your old nature just won't want to do that. Many times I feel that tug like an actual pain inside of me, and the decision to think correctly doesn't come easily. It may be a struggle that lasts a moment or hours or days.

The longer you allow this struggle with a wrong thought to continue, the more likely you are to make the wrong decision. Jesus told us to cut off our hand if it offends us, or pluck out our eye if it offends us (Matt. 5:29-30). Once we see something offensive—once we know that garbage is trying to get into our minds—we need to be prepared for drastic action if necessary, and we need to move as quickly as possible. The longer we wait to make the right decision, the more opportunity we give our enemy to keep tempting us and trying to make us fail.

I hope I've been able to help you see how important it is to keep the garbage of this world out of your mind. Controlling the input into your mind is a key element in bringing your thoughts into line with Philippians 4:8.

Memorizing Scripture

Psalm 119:11 says: "I have hidden your word in my heart that I might not sin against you." Remembering that *heart* here refers to our minds, as we discussed in chapter 1, the psalmist has given us some wonderful advice for thought control: hiding God's Word in our mind. If Scripture memorization scares you, then don't use that term. Think instead of hiding the truth of God's Word in the recesses of your minds. Whether or not you hide it word for word, that hidden Word, tucked away for a mentally rainy day, will prove to be a great help at that point when you know you should screen out a wrong thought but the process seems particularly difficult.

I'm so thankful for the Christian upbringing I had that encouraged me to memorize passages of the Bible from the time I could talk. Every Sunday we had our memory verse to quote, and my mother would usually check on Saturdays to see if I had completed my Sunday School lesson for the next day.

I imagine my Sunday School teachers were often discouraged when they were trying to teach us those verses. I'm sure there were days when they wondered if it made any difference to drum these Bible verses into those little heads, those sometimes inattentive and unenthusiastic heads. But I'm so glad they made me hide God's Word in my mind because the Holy Spirit can and often does bring His Word out of the recesses of my mind at just the right moment to instruct me, to encourage me, to convict me, to keep me on the right path.

We learn the power of God's hidden Word in our minds from the example of Jesus when He was tempted by Satan. Three times the Enemy tried to lure Jesus into his trap, but each time Jesus was victorious. He knew Satan's tricks and didn't fall for them. And His weapon was the hidden Word of God. Notice how He answered each one of Satan's three temptations:

> Jesus answered, "It is written, 'Man does not live on bread alone, but on every word that comes from the mouth of God.'"
>
> Matt. 4:4

Jesus answered him, "It is also written: 'Do not put the

Lord your God to the test.'"

Matt. 4:7

Jesus said to him, "Away from me, Satan! For it is written: 'Worship the Lord your God, and serve him only.'"

Matt. 4:10

Jesus did not have the written Word of God with Him out there in the desert during this temptation. In fact, the written Word of God was only in the temple and tabernacles in those days. No one had a private copy. But Jesus knew God's Word; it was hidden in His mind, where no one could take it from Him. So when He needed it, it was there to defeat the Enemy.

You may be thinking, yes, but that was Jesus. Don't forget that while Jesus was totally and fully God, He was also totally and fully man, experiencing all the temptations that we experience. (See Heb. 4:15.) So, He was tempted to fall for Satan's tricks. He had to make a decision at the point of temptation whether or not to give in. Keep in mind, Jesus was very hungry and very weak after forty days of fasting, and His flesh no doubt found some of Satan's suggestions very attractive. But He did not answer that phone call, even though Satan dialed His number and rang His bell. He didn't answer because the Word of God was hidden in His heart; therefore, He did not sin.

The same principle is true for each of us. So, whether you memorize word for word or not, hide God's Word in your mind. One good method for doing that is singing choruses and songs that are based on Scripture. I find I can remember the words to a song very easily. So, sing God's Word into your mind. In any Christian bookstore you'll find cassette tapes or CDs full of passages of Scripture put to music. Buy several and learn to sing these songs. Listen to such music while you're driving, and you can fortify your mind and build up spiritual muscle in time that you otherwise might have wasted.

Another method for Scripture memorization is to put verses and passages on cards and keep them in view, reading and rereading them often. If you read a passage many, many times, it will become hidden in your mind. So, put verses of Scripture on the refrigerator door, on the dashboard of your car, propped up on your desk, on your calendar, type them on your computer screen saver, tape them to your bathroom mirror. Those frequent visual reminders will continually fill your mind with the truth of God's Word, and you will find it much easier to hang up on the wrong thoughts.

My pastor told of an experience he had in counseling a young man who had been consumed by lustful and impure thoughts for many years. He had become addicted to pornography and just couldn't seem to stay away from it. (Another example of how wrong input into his mind controlled his thinking.) He had accepted Christ and wanted to be rid of this horrible problem, but he was finding it very difficult.

Our pastor gave him a list of verses to memorize, pertaining to purity of life. Verses like "Blessed are the pure in heart, for they will see God" (Matt. 5:8). Another was "Create in me a pure heart, O God, and renew a steadfast spirit within me" (Ps. 51:10).

My pastor counseled this young man first to burn all his pornographic material and not allow any of it into his home. Then, when he felt tempted to go to a store to either look at or buy pornographic material, the pastor told him to repeat his verses ten times each. Even if he found himself headed toward the store, he was to start repeating the verses, out loud if possible, ten times each.

Since he sincerely wanted to break this habit, this young

man agreed to follow the pastor's suggestions. So, when the temptation to go find some pornographic material began to obsess him, he would start reciting, "Blessed are the pure in heart, for they will see God. Blessed are the pure in heart, for they will see God. Blessed are the pure in heart, for they will see God." And when he said that one ten times, he started reciting the other verses.

He quickly discovered that the power of Scripture was stronger than his obsession, and by reciting those verses, he was able to change his thinking and avoid the pornography. And each time he avoided pornography, he became spiritually stronger. He began to build spiritual muscle, which gave him more strength to resist the next time of temptation.

We must all follow this young man's example and reprogram our minds, building spiritual muscle for those moments of decision when a wrong thought rings our phone and we must decide whether or not to take the call.

Avoid Messy Cleanup

Years ago when I first began to practice this discipline of screening my thoughts and paying attention to what I was thinking, I remember coming home from work one evening with the intention of getting some writing done. It was in the early years of my radio program, and I needed to prepare for a recording session. I turned the television on to catch the nightly news with the intention of turning it off as soon as the news ended. I didn't flick the switch quickly enough, however, and I allowed myself to start watching a television movie.

Before I knew it, I was watching this movie with interest. While it would not be classified as X-rated, it certainly did not have an edifying story line. As I remember, it had something to do with an adulterous affair. The Spirit of Christ within me gave me a warning; I knew I should turn it off. But I didn't. So I wasted two hours watching garbage, didn't accomplish the writing I needed to do, and filled my mind with images that were not true, noble, right, pure, lovely, or admirable.

The next day at work I couldn't get that movie out of my mind. It kept coming back at the strangest times. I noticed that when I tried to pray, scenes from the movie would invade my mind. It took several days to get that garbage cleaned out of my mind.

I remember thinking, *It's not worth it. Putting garbage into my mind creates such a mess that takes so long to clean up. I can't afford to do this anymore.* From that point on when I was tempted to watch something that I knew would not pass the Philippians 4:8 test, I would remind myself of the cleanup that would be required. It was a good lesson to learn. I still remind myself that it's simply not worth it to allow trash into my mind because sooner or later I'm going to have to clean out my mind, and that is a painful and difficult process.

Think About It

Reading Habits

Think about what you've read in the last thirty days. Make a list of your reading material and estimate the amount of time you've spent on each type of material.

In the last thirty days I've read these books: Time involved:

_____   _____

_____   _____

_____   _____

_____   _____

_____   _____

_____   _____

_____   _____

In the last thirty days I've read these magazines:

_____   _____

_____   _____

_____   _____

_____   _____

_____   _____

_____   _____

In the last thirty days I've read these newspapers:

_____   _____

_____   _____

_____   _____

_____   _____

_____   _____

_____   _____

_____   _____

TOTAL TIME   _____

What was your total estimated reading time?

Now, go back and put a G beside anything you read that you would now classify as garbage. If you have one or more G on your list, determine to eliminate that item from your reading this month.

Now, think about how much time you spent reading your Bible over that same thirty-day period. Enter that total here:

_____

Do you need to change your reading habits? If so, what will you do?

Viewing Habits

Now, think of what has recently been poured into your mind through movies and television.

In the last fourteen days I've watched:

Movies (include video rentals)   Television Sitcoms

_____	_____
_____	_____
_____	_____
_____	_____
_____	_____
_____	_____
_____	_____
_____	_____
_____	_____
_____	_____
_____	_____
_____	_____
_____	_____
_____	_____
_____	_____
_____	_____
_____	_____

Television Soap Operas   News Programs/Other

_____   _____
_____   _____
_____   _____
_____   _____
_____   _____
_____   _____
_____   _____
_____   _____
_____   _____
_____   _____
_____   _____
_____   _____
_____   _____
_____   _____
_____   _____

Now, here's the hard part. Put a P beside any items on your list above that would pass our Philippians 4:8 test: True, noble, right, pure, lovely, and admirable.

What do you need to do so that every item on your viewing list next month can be labeled with a P?

Listening Habits

What kind of conversations do you listen to? For instance, what do you usually hear going on around you on your job? Check any descriptions that apply to you.

__ Negative conversations
__ Critical conversations
__ Off-color jokes
__ Sexual innuendoes
__ Gossip

Here are some specific examples of a few types of such conversations. Think of something you could say or do to either avoid or redirect each of these remarks if they occurred in your presence.

You hear this: "There's no need even asking if you can get some help for that project. You know nobody ever listens to anything we have to say. Nobody cares if things get done right here or not."

You might say this:

_____

_____

_____

_____

_____

You hear this: "Listen, our boss is not on top of this. Frankly, I don't think he even knows what he's doing. When I asked him about the Matthews Case yesterday, he got very flustered because he couldn't answer my question. He's just not very bright, you know."

You might say this:

_____

_____

_____

_____

_____

You hear this: "Hey, I heard this new joke last night. It's about a salesman who meets this girl . . ."

You might say this:

_____

_____

_____

_____

_____

Consider these questions about the conversations you hear: When is it appropriate to walk away from a conversation?

Which is more important: protecting someone else's feelings or keeping his or her improper and/or impure conversations from getting into your mind?

What message do we send to nonbelievers when we go along with their inappropriate conversations and act as though we have no problem with them?

As you are doing the hard work of changing some of your habits, don't forget to pray Philippians 4:8 into your life each day.

Lord,

Help me today to think only what is true, noble, right, pure, lovely, and admirable. Make me aware of any thoughts that do not meet these criteria. Give me both the desire and the will to change my thoughts because I know that what I think is what I am.

In Jesus' name,

Amen.

Chapter 9

THE REPLACEMENT

PRINCIPLE

Here is one of the most unusual illustrations that Jesus, the Master Teacher, ever gave:

When an evil spirit comes out of a man, it goes through arid places seeking rest and does not find it. Then it says, 'I will return to the house I left.' When it arrives, it finds the house swept clean and put in order. Then it goes and takes seven other spirits more wicked than itself, and they go in and live there. And the final condition of that man is worse than the first.

Luke 11:24-26

You'll find this illustration repeated almost word for word

in Matthew 12:43-45. This is certainly not an easy teaching to understand. It almost seems to say that it is an exercise in futility to get rid of evil spirits because they will return to the person they left and bring more evil spirits with them. But that interpretation would not be consistent with the whole of Scripture because we know that Jesus frequently cast out evil spirits and encouraged His disciples to do so as well.

I believe one of the things Jesus is teaching us in this story is that evil spirits should come out of a person, but if the evil is not replaced with good, that person is vulnerable to even greater evil. Vacuums in our hearts and minds are susceptible to evil influences. When the evil is cast out, therefore, it needs to be replaced with good so that the evil will not be able to reinvade the heart and mind from which it was cast out. I have named this the Replacement Principle, and I believe it is an essential element for all those who are serious about getting their thought life under control.

The preceding chapters of this book have focused on the importance of cleaning out the garbage and keeping it from entering our minds. But after our mental houses have been cleaned up, after we've hung up the phone on the wrong thoughts, we must then fill up those same mental houses with the right thoughts in order to protect ourselves from the ever present evil that seeks to reenter our minds.

Our Enemy will certainly not give up trying to control our minds, and when he sees we are serious about cleaning out the wrong thoughts, he will redouble his efforts to come back and occupy our renewed minds with even more evil thoughts. But when he returns to bombard our minds with wrong thinking, if he finds our minds are occupied and filled up with the right kind of thoughts, he is prevented from moving in again.

It is extremely important that we understand and apply this Replacement Principle, which is simply replacing a wrong thought with a right thought. As soon as we hang up the phone on the wrong thought that has tried to enter our mind, we must switch from the negative to the positive and consciously replace that wrong thought with a right one. It is not enough to know that a particular thought pattern is wrong; we must also make a fast decision to replace it with a thought pattern that is right. That prevents the wrong thoughts from coming back because the empty house is now full with good thoughts, leaving no room for the wrong ones.

So, in order to be prepared to practice this Replacement Principle, it is very helpful to establish in advance the right thought patterns, the replacement thoughts, we can use to fill up our mental houses. We need spiritual reflexes that come to our aid quickly. That's what I'd like to cover in this chapter.

Our Basic Reflex Replacement Thought

The Bible gives us this reflex thought that will work for us every time: "You will keep him in perfect peace, whose mind is stayed on You, because he trusts in You" (Isa. 26:3 NKJV). The "You" referred to in this verse is, of course, the Lord God.

Hebrews 3:1 tells us: "Therefore, holy brothers, who share in the heavenly calling, fix your minds on Jesus, the apostle and high priest whom we confess."

This reflex replacement thought represented in these verses will work in any situation; it is a generic, all-purpose thought pattern that any of us can use for any mental dilemma in which we find ourselves. It is so simple that we can overlook it or complicate it or fail to take it seriously. But God's Word urges us to keep our minds fixed on the Lord Jesus Christ. When you need to fill your mind with good thoughts, just think about Jesus.

Think about all that Jesus suffered to bring you salvation.

Think about how He now is seated at God's right hand, ever living to make intercession for you. Think about how He left heaven's glory and all that was rightly His to come to earth and become sin for you. Just start thinking about Jesus. Any thoughts you have of Him will be effective in replacing whatever wrong thoughts you have just banished.

If you are frightened, thoughts of Jesus will fill your mind with peace. If you are tired, thoughts of Jesus will renew your strength. If you are worried, thinking of Jesus will bring you courage and confidence. If you are angry, Jesus will fill you up with compassion and comfort. None of us can ever have an excuse for not replacing the wrong thoughts with right ones because we can always think about Jesus. He is always our sure Deliverer.

Replacing Specific Wrong Thoughts

Let's dig deeper into God's Word to find even more specific passages that we can store in our minds for those emergency replacement thoughts. As we take a look at these different categories, focus in on the one or ones with which you have the most difficulty. Thankfully, not all of us have problems in all areas. I know where my major weaknesses are, and those are the areas where I must be faithful to "do my homework" and hide God's Word in my heart so that the enemy of my soul will not be successful when he tries to invade my mind again and again.

Don't lose sight of the incredible power we have when we apply God's Word directly to our situation. The writer to the Hebrews told us:

The word of God is living and active. Sharper than any double-edged sword, it penetrates even to dividing soul and spirit, joints and marrow; it judges the thoughts and attitudes of the heart.

Heb. 4:12

As we learn from Ephesians 6, God's Word is the only offensive weapon in our arsenal with which we can defeat our enemy, but it is the only one we need. We must, however, learn how to apply the Word of God directly to our minds, with specific Scriptures for different areas of need.

Following are some of the more common areas where our thoughts easily wander off the frozen surface to the bushes and mud, with some suggested Scriptures we can store in our minds in advance to use as replacements.

We can replace untrue thoughts.

A great many of our untrue thoughts are fearful thoughts, worrying and wondering about what might happen, what tragedy could descend upon us, what could go wrong. As we discussed in chapter 3, those are always untrue thoughts.

All of us have pockets of fear, areas where we struggle more to be able to trust God. If you think of some of the great people of the Bible, you will recognize that many of them had their pockets of fear. Abraham was afraid of running out of food, so he left God's beaten path and went to Egypt. Then he was afraid he would be killed because his wife, Sarah, was so beautiful (strange thinking!). So, he lied to protect his life.

How could such a man of faith, who was willing to leave everything and go to a land that he'd never been to, have such pockets of fear? It would seem that if he could trust God in those other areas of his life, he'd be able to trust God to supply his food and protect his life. But Abraham had pockets of fear. All of us do.

What is your pocket of fear? It might be fear of being alone, fear of what others are saying about you, fear that you'll lose your job, or fear that your marriage will break up. If you can specifically identify any areas of fear in your life, you will then be in a much better position to start defeating and replacing those fearful thoughts.

While fearful thoughts are not my biggest problem, one verse I use when I start to feel fearful is "When I am afraid, I will trust in you" (Ps. 56:3). I just repeat it over and over. Remember, we have to set our will to trust God, right in the midst of those fearful feelings.

Living alone as I do—and as probably many of you do, too—I occasionally find myself gripped with fear as I hear some sound in the night that convinces me someone is breaking into my home. This doesn't happen to me very often, but I can remember lying in bed one night, stiff with fear, as I listened to noises. And my mind started imagining what was going to happen to me. The fear was so strong that I literally couldn't move—my legs and arms were paralyzed. But I could quote Scripture, so I started quoting, "When I am afraid, I will trust in you." Soon, I was able to get out of bed, check out the problem, assure myself nothing was wrong, and go back to sleep. The Word of God broke the stronghold of fear because I replaced a wrong thought with a right one.

Here are some other great passages to help us replace those fearful thoughts:

Do not be afraid of those who kill the body but cannot kill the soul. Rather, be afraid of the one who can destroy both soul and body in hell. Are not two sparrows sold for a penny? Yet not one of them will fall to the ground apart from the will of your Father. And even the very hairs of your head are all numbered. So don't be afraid; you are worth more than many sparrows.

Matt. 10:28-31

The Lord is my light and my salvation—whom shall I fear? The Lord is the stronghold of my life—of whom shall I be afraid? When evil men advance against me to devour my flesh, when my enemies and my foes attack me, they will stumble and fall. Though an army besiege me, my heart will not fear; though war break out against me, even then will I be confident.

Ps. 27:1-3

Strengthen the feeble hands, steady the knees that give way; say to those with fearful hearts, "Be strong, do not fear; your God will come, he will come with vengeance; with divine retribution he will come to save you."

Isa. 35:3-4

When fear starts to overtake us, we can use these passages to replace our wrong thinking with thoughts about God's great power and His promises to take care of us. These would be some good verses to memorize if fearful thoughts are a struggle for you. That way, when fear starts to take over your mind, you can quote some of these verses, and they will drive out the wrong, fearful thoughts as you are reminded of God's care for you.

One paraphrase of Hebrews 12:3 reminds us: "Think constantly of him [Jesus Christ] enduring all that sinful men could say against him and you will not lose your purpose or your courage" (PH).

When we start to think about what Jesus did for us and how much He endured for us, it gives us the courage we need to face our thoughts of fear and by the power of God, cast them out. John tells us that "There is no fear in love. But perfect love drives out fear, because fear has to do with punishment" (1 John 4:18). Thinking about the love of God which is given to us will drive out the thoughts of fear—any kind of fear.

Remember that God never gives us a spirit of fear: "For you did not receive a spirit that makes you a slave again to fear, but you received the Spirit of sonship. And by him we cry, 'Abba, Father'" (Rom. 8:15). And in 2 Timothy we read: "For God did not give us a spirit of fear, but of power and of love and of a sound mind" (2 Tim. 1:7, NKJV).

Any time we feel fearful, it is certain that the Enemy is attacking us, and it is a sign that we are not trusting God. Fear and trust cannot coexist. So, when fear starts to overtake our minds, we must go to Scriptures that remind us to trust and renew our minds with a spirit of power, of love, of sonship.

We can replace thoughts that are not noble.

Thoughts that criticize and judge others, as we discussed in chapter 4, may be true, but they are never noble. We have strong directives in Scripture that teach us not to have a judgmental spirit. Nothing crushes people more than judgment and criticism. Keep reminding yourself that the critical things that come out of your mouth begin in your mind. If you stop the thinking, you'll stop the words.

Jesus gives us some strong words about being a judgmental person: "Do not judge, or you too will be judged. For in the same way you judge others, you will be judged, and with the measure you use, it will be measured to you" (Matt. 7:1-2). Doesn't that frighten you a bit to think that you will be judged by the same standards you judge others? That alone should drive us away from judgmental thinking.

Here's another good reference to use as a replacement thought for judgmental thinking:

You, then, why do you judge your brother? Or why do you look down on your brother? For we will all stand before God's judgment seat. It is written: "'As surely as I live,' says the Lord, 'every knee will bow before me; every tongue will confess to God.'" So then, each of us will give an account of himself to God. Therefore let us stop passing judgment on one another. Instead, make up your mind not to put any stumbling block or obstacle in your brother's way.

Rom. 14:10-13

Isn't it amazing how often the very thing we criticize others for is an area in which we fail quite frequently? I suppose it's just easier for us to see mistakes in others than in ourselves. It's a good idea, when you find yourself thinking critical or judgmental thoughts of others, to stop and say to yourself, "You know, I do the same thing. Who do I think I am to criticize other people? I am just as guilty of this as they are." It's almost always true. And if we're not guilty of the same type of offense, we need to stop those proud thoughts about how much better we are than others!

We can replace impure thoughts.

Impure and immoral thinking is at such high levels in our society that all of us need to be very cautious in this area. This immoral thinking is due to the fact, of course, that society has exploited sex in every way possible. Please be aware that no one is immune to this type of impure and immoral thinking.

Here is what the Bible teaches us about purifying our thoughts:

Dear friends, now we are children of God, and what we will be has not yet been made known. But we know that when he appears, we shall be like him, for we shall see him as he is. Everyone who has this hope in him purifies himself, just as he is pure.

1 John 3:2-3

Why does the knowledge of Jesus' second coming cause us to be pure? Well, think of when you were a child. If Mom and Dad were out of the house for a few hours, you felt you could break some of the rules. Maybe you weren't supposed to eat candy, but with Mom away, you'd go for the candy dish. Or she told you to clean your room, but since she wasn't there, you didn't bother.

But when you were anticipating the imminent return of your parents, it would often motivate you to get busy and do what you were supposed to do—or stop doing what you were not supposed to do. Your sibling might have come running into the room shouting, "Mom's coming! Mom's coming! Hurry, let's get this stuff put away." And like a white tornado, you'd try to get it all done before Mom made her way into the house. That kind of anticipation was based on fear, for the most part. You were afraid of what was going to happen when Mom or Dad arrived.

By the same token, if we live in anticipation of the fact that Jesus could appear at any time, that will affect our thinking and our behavior in similar ways. I hope that anticipation will be based on love and a desire to please our Savior. But quite frankly, a little holy fear wouldn't hurt any of us. We need to have a reverential fear of the consequences we face from a Holy God.

When impure thoughts start to move in, start thinking about the second coming of Jesus Christ. Talk to yourself about how we're going to be like Him when He appears. Let your mind dwell on the great hope of the Second Coming. That is a good cure for impure thinking.

We can replace unlovely thoughts.

When we start to feel sorry for ourselves and organize a

pity party, our thoughts are immediately in the "unlovely" category. The Bible gives us an absolutely perfect way to fill up our minds with right thinking and keep self-pity from coming back.

Thankfulness is a sure cure for self-pity. Start reciting all you have to be thankful for and self-pity has to stop. If possible, count your blessings out loud so your ears have to hear what your mind is saying. First Thessalonians 5:18 reminds us, "Give thanks in all circumstances, for this is God's will for you in Christ Jesus."

I remember experiencing a disappointment when I didn't get something I wanted, something I thought I needed, and I thought my motives were good, since I wanted to use it in God's service. But, after getting very close, it was denied to me. I found myself starting in with the self-pity immediately:

> I don't understand this, Lord. Why would you let me get so close and then take it away from me? That seems cruel. After all, I don't ask for so much, do I? Was it such a big deal that I should have this thing? Furthermore, I just wanted it to help out in the ministry. And nobody else seems to care that I've been disappointed. They all just take it nonchalantly, without any sympathy, giving me platitudes like "Well, you just have to take it from the Lord."

At that point I was beginning to learn the great joy that comes when I do replace the wrong thoughts with the right ones. So, as soon as I recognized the self-pity, I began to list all the things I had to be thankful for. I read a couple of letters from listeners who have had real tragedies in their lives and reminded myself that what I was experiencing was simply a disappointment, not a tragedy. I recounted all the many good things God has done for me and remembered that after all, I'm a servant. Servants don't make demands; servants are obedient. And I recited verses that tell me that my God has plans for me that are good, not evil, and whatever He does is for my good.

By replacing the self-pity thoughts with thankful thoughts, I was able to keep the self-pity out. I didn't do it because I felt like doing it, however. In fact, my feelings hardly changed. I didn't jump up and down and say, "Oh, isn't it wonderful I've had this great disappointment." But I did have that inner peace of knowing that God has a purpose, and I can trust Him.

Over a period of a few days, I had to replace those self-pity thoughts several times. It's not once and for all, you know. But it works; it really works.

We can replace thoughts that are not admirable.

Romans 12:3 tells us:

> For by the grace given me I say to every one of you: Do not think of yourself more highly than you ought, but rather think of yourself with sober judgment, in accordance with the measure of faith God has given you.

It's easy to find ourselves immersed in proud thinking about ourselves, our accomplishments, our talents and abilities. Those are not admirable thoughts; they are not thoughts to be admired. Here are some antidotes for proud thinking:

> For who makes you different from anyone else? What do you have that you did not receive? And if you did receive it, why do you boast as though you did not?
>
> 1 Cor. 4:7

Your attitude should be the same as that of Christ

Jesus: Who, being in very nature God, did not consider equality with God something to be grasped, but made himself nothing, taking the very nature of a servant, being made in human likeness. And being found in appearance as a man, he humbled himself and became obedient to death—even death on a cross!

Phil. 2:5-8

It was Jesus' right to be equal with God and enjoy all that God had. Yet, He was willing to become a servant and be made like a human man. And He demonstrated the ultimate in humility when He was willing to die on a cross in obedience to God. This humble attitude of Jesus is to be our attitude, Paul tells us. So, when we start thinking we're pretty "hot stuff," all we need to do is start thinking about Who Jesus is and how He was willing to humble Himself. Then we need to remind ourselves of 1 Corinthians 4, which says we have nothing that wasn't given to us; therefore, how can we be proud of a gift or act as though we can take credit for it.

If I had to identify my toughest area of wrong thinking, I would have to admit that I struggle with proud thoughts more than anything else. The passages of Scripture I've referred to concerning proud thoughts have been a great help to me.

When I receive compliments about something I've done, pride can start to move in pretty quickly. I can find myself thinking dumb things like *You really do that very well.* Or when I see someone else teaching or speaking, I can find myself thinking, *I could have said that better,* or *This person really isn't presenting this material very well.* That's when I bring 1 Corinthians 4 to mind and remind myself that whatever gifts I have are no credit of my own. And Philippians 2:5-8 has frequently helped me bring these proud thoughts under control. Just to think about Jesus and how He humbled

Himself for us makes it impossible to continue to think about yourself in a proud way.

I remember Corrie ten Boom telling how she handled the many compliments and flattering things that people said to her. At the end of each day when her head had been filled with all those nice comments, she simply gathered them all together as a mental bouquet and gave them back to Jesus. I've often used that as a guide for myself, just giving back to God the good things said to me, things that could make me proud or cause me to start to take credit myself. It's a great way to remind yourself that everything you have is a gift and that you cannot allow proud thoughts to get started.

The Moment of Decision

I don't mean to imply that it's always easy to replace wrong thoughts. It isn't. The moment of abandoning the wrong thought and forcing myself to think correctly is a moment of struggle in my mind. And sometimes I have to replace wrong thoughts every minute or two. But don't let that discourage you. Keep applying this principle. Just keep replacing. You're changing habits that are ingrained, and you're in a warfare with your enemy. So, don't give up; just replace the wrong thought with the right thought, as many times as necessary.

Think About It

In order to practice the Replacement Principle in your own life, prepare yourself by recognizing the areas in which you have the greatest struggles in your thought life.

What kind of thoughts do you find the most difficult to get out of your mind? Check all that apply.

___ Fearful thoughts of the future
___ Fearful thoughts of failure
___ Worrying about my finances
___ Feeling guilty without reason
___ Excessive daydreaming/fantasies
___ Critical and judgmental thoughts
___ Negative thinking
___ Thoughts of retribution
___ Impure sexual thoughts
___ Prejudicial thoughts
___ Self-pity thoughts
___ Proud thoughts

Find a passage in the Bible that will be an antidote for the impure thoughts you checked. Many suggestions have been given in this chapter as well as the specific chapters that covered each of these kinds of thoughts. Or use a Bible concordance to find some verses of your own. If you dig them out for yourself, they will be much more meaningful to you.

Put each verse or passage you find on a separate card that you can easily carry with you. Better still, memorize those passages. The more familiar you are with these verses, the easier it will be to replace the wrong thoughts with the right ones.

Chapter 10

THE REWARDS FOR

BIBLICAL THINKING

O ne of the values we seem to have lost in the last couple of generations is that of delayed rewards. With our incredible fixation on speed, we want everything now. We've really bought into instant gratification.

For fifteen years I've been conducting business seminars for a major business education company, taking me all across this country, to every major city, speaking to thousands of people. I remember one young man who approached me at one of these seminars to ask how he could become a speaker like me. He was in his early twenties and had only been in his career a short time. But he felt he could do a good job making presentations, and he was ready to embark on a new career.

I explained that the most important ingredient of a business presentation is credibility. Then I told him of the years I spent in several jobs that have given me the experience and knowledge I need to stand in front of thousands of businesspeople and be an effective trainer. In essence, I told him he would need to gain some years of experience before he would be equipped to do what I was doing.

My response irritated him. He was not happy to hear that he needed to earn the position he wanted, and I'm certain he was convinced that I was wrong. He let me know that he could do my job without any difficulty, and he could not understand why experience and time would make any difference.

His was not an untypical reaction. Many people have asked me similar questions, thinking my job looked fun and fairly easy. A message of "put in your time and build your credentials" is not music to anyone's ears.

Think about it. Isn't this fairly symptomatic of our entire society? We often sacrifice the long-term for the immediate. I'm beginning to realize how much this world system can subtly control my thinking because I often find myself in that instant gratification mode. It is a struggle to remind myself that some things—the best things—come with waiting.

That is somewhat true when we think of the rewards that are ours when we learn and practice these principles of biblical thinking. Struggling to train our minds may seem like a very ungratifying exercise. But the delayed rewards are so huge, so all-pervasive, so life-changing, that if ever anything was worth working and waiting for, this is it!

The Reward of Life and Peace

If you got down to the real bottom line, what is it people today truly want? People would express themselves in different ways and words, but I think most people would agree on two items: life and peace. We all want life—fulfillment, happiness, excitement, meaningful activity. And we all want peace—contentment, restfulness, lack of stress and worry, tranquillity. Life and peace.

That's exactly what right thinking brings into our lives. As Paul tells us in Romans 8:6 (NASB): "For the mind set on the flesh is death, but the mind set on the Spirit is life and peace."

If we know that we have life and peace, what else do we really need? And we see here in Romans 8:6 that we can have life and peace when our minds are set on the Spirit of God—when our minds are consumed with pleasing God, and when we are committed to having our minds controlled by His Spirit.

Life and peace. You can't buy them, you can't earn them, you can't manufacture them. But they are yours for right thinking. So, as difficult as it may appear at first, the rewards for cleaning up our thought lives are well worth the discipline required.

The Reward of a Transformed Life

In my opinion and experience, one of the most important and life-changing passages in the whole Bible is Romans 12:1-2:

> Therefore, I urge you, brothers, in view of God's mercy, to offer your bodies as living sacrifices, holy and pleasing to God—which is your spiritual worship. Do not conform any longer to the pattern of this world, but be transformed by the renewing of your mind. Then you will be able to test and approve what God's will is—His good, pleasing and perfect will.

You and I can be transformed people. I'm serious. When you earnestly begin to renew your mind through right thinking, you will see changes in yourself that you would never have believed possible.

As I write this chapter, I am reminded of two recent situations in which God showed me the power of right thinking to change lives—especially my own life. A few months ago I spent ten days on a missions trip to Kenya, Africa with eight wonderful women from Indiana, women I had never met until we rendezvoused in Kenya. Nine women in one van over bumpy roads, with not always the best accommodations, food, or facilities—that's a recipe for conflict! But we had a wonderful opportunity to minister to some special women in Kenya, and God gave us sweet fellowship together.

Toward the end of our time together, the women said to me something like "You've been so patient on this trip and so quiet." Patient and quiet? Me? I couldn't believe my ears. In fact, I jokingly asked if they would sign an affidavit to that effect so I could prove to my friends back home that someone had called me patient and quiet. Believe me, that is not the natural person named Mary Whelchel.

Yet, as I thought about their kind words, the Spirit of God reminded me that for quite a few years now I have diligently been praying for a transformed life, for changes that I knew needed to be made in me. And I have specifically prayed that God would make me more patient, as well as quick to listen and slow to speak. So, in a special moment for me, God confirmed that He still answers prayer and that He is very capable of transforming me, even to making me patient and quiet— well, at least more patient and quiet than I was before!

In another setting a few weeks later, some women thanked me for my sweet spirit and repeatedly mentioned how my sweet spirit had ministered to them. Sweet spirit? Again, that is not the old Mary Whelchel. *Sweet* is never a word I have associated with myself. But I serve a transforming God, and He is willing to transform me into the image of Jesus Christ with ever increasing glory:

> And we, who with unveiled faces all reflect the Lord's glory, are being transformed into his likeness with ever-increasing glory, which comes from the Lord, who is the Spirit.
>
> 2 Cor. 3:18

I guess to many people those examples would sound like very small victories. Why would they mean so much to me? Because I know what I was like before; I know I could never change myself; and I'm thrilled to see God's power at work in my life when I am obedient and disciplined to follow His principles of right thinking.

Of course, there is much left to be changed in my life. I've only just begun to see this transformation take place, and I wish it were greater and faster. But even so, I am excited to see some evidence of a transformed life—a transformation that began as I started learning and practicing the principles of right thinking that I've communicated in this book.

The Result of Practice

I can testify that right thinking becomes more attractive the more you practice it. I remember recently starting to get into some self-pity thoughts. You know, the "poor me" syndrome. And I caught myself and stopped because I did not want to have self-pity. I said to myself, "I don't want to be depressed. I don't want to be blue or down. I will not think these self-pity thoughts."

Those same thoughts which I readily indulged in before

were now distasteful to me. I had enough experience at changing my thinking to realize how much better it is not to indulge in self-pity thinking. Isn't it amazing! God really knows what He's talking about. And He always has our best interests at heart. So, applying His principles, as difficult as they may appear at times, is always for our good.

Committing to Jesus on the Highest Level

Are you hungry to see some transformations in your life? Perhaps you feel weighed down with sins and attitudes that you cannot shake. Are you are often overcome with depression and loneliness? Maybe you suffer from frequent periods of dreariness and boredom. It could be that anger and bitterness eat you up on the inside.

Whatever changes are on your wish list, you can be transformed if, first, you are a born-again believer as defined by God's Word and, second, you are willing to bring all your thoughts into captivity and make them obedient to Christ. Now that you've explored what that means and how to do it in depth, you have come to a decision point.

Will you take the necessary steps to begin walking down the very promising road of transformed thinking? Don't be fooled by the world's false promises. Freedom comes when our thoughts become captive to Jesus Christ. Truth sets us free, and this is truth.

You've learned some important truths in this book. But remember that the blessing is in the doing, not in the knowing. In fact, knowing and not doing means you will be judged more severely.

I hope by now you've begun the process of bringing your thoughts into line with Philippians 4:8. But you and I will never be through learning this principle of controlling our thoughts. It is a daily lesson that involves a continually changing lifestyle. When you practice it seriously, it is a commitment to Jesus Christ on the highest level. Your thoughts control you; therefore, they need to be controlled by the Spirit of God within you.

This is meant to be the normal life of every Christian, but few are ever willing to take God at His Word and work at letting Him control their thoughts. I can testify to you, as one who is still learning this principle, that it will make a wonderful difference in your life. It's well worth the price you will pay.

If you liked this book,
   check out these great titles from
      ChariotVICTOR Publishing . . .

Found: God's Will
by John MacArthur
ISBN 1-56476-740-X

Bible teacher John MacArthur answers six key
questions about God's will asked by most
Christians at one time or another. This short,
digest-style book is as pertinent today as it was
when it was first published 25 years ago.

And this title by Mary Whelchel . . .

If You Only Knew
by Mary Whelchel
ISBN: 1-56476-605-5

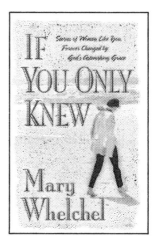

Explore the lives of both biblical women and
modern-day women who have struggled to
find meaning and purpose in life. It is a
message of hope for women today, showing
that nothing can disqualify them from God's
astonishing grace.